DUDLEY

Ned Williams

URALIA PRESS

1994

Uralia Press: 23 Westland Road, Wolverhampton, WV3 9NZ

On the front cover: Approximately a quarter of a century separates the two pictures, taken in about the same spot, as trains reach the summit of their long climb from Great Bridge, pass under the Dudley-Tipton road and turn into the northern end of Dudley Station, or the site of it. About 1963, an ex LMS class 5 4-6-0 locomotive, no. 44812 (of Saltley shed), arrives at Dudley with the afternoon Derby - Bristol parcels train, as Signalman M.Willis looks on from the window of Dudley East signal box. Although Dudley Station had spent most of its life as a frontier between separate sections of the railway system, these inter-regional workings were a feature of its final years, and this train was routed via Dudley and over ex Western tracks rather than take the ex Midland route via Lickey. (Photo: John Harris)

The lower picture was taken in October 1989 and records a class 47 diesel locomotive passing much the same spot with a Stoke - St. Blazey train of empty china clay wagons. Signal box and station have gone, the Freightliner Depot has come and gone, and Dudley "Station" spent the last few years of its life as a rather featureless spot on a little used railway. (Brian Robbins)

On the back cover: Parkhead Viaduct, just south of Blowers Green, was one of the most dramatic features of Dudley's varied railway landscape. The vicinity included canals, locks, lock-keeper's cottages, a canal tunnel, the railway and viaduct, an engine house and all manner of industrial activity. In this picture, the Severn Valley Railways's preserved Stanier 8F 2-8-0, 8233, passes over the viaduct on its way to Derby. In the foreground is a landscape restored and "preserved" by British Waters, the local authority and the Dudley Canal Tunnel Trust. (Photo: Bob Green)

Lower back cover: NCB Hunslet 0-6-0ST no.9 (3777 of 1952), photographed at Baggeridge Colliery - looking towards the pit - in 1965. Behind the engine is a "P.R." wagon (Pensnett Railway) because, at this time, coal was still leaving the pit to be taken down to Askew Bridge to be handed over to one of the Round Oak Steel Works diesel locomotives to be transported to the steel works. (Roger Crombleholme)

Frontispiece: BR Standard class 9F 2-10-0, no. 92026 leaves Dudley beneath the Birmingham Road Bridge in 1965 with the Crewe - Stoke Gifford freight that had worked via the Wombourn route until that line's closure at the end of February of that year. (John Harris)

The Railways of Dudley

ISBN 1 898 528 02 0

Published by Uralia Press
Wolverhampton 1994

Photographic prints made by Jan Endean
Screened for publication by Galata Print
Page origination by Uralia Press
Cover design and track layouts by
Roger Crombleholme (Alphagraphix)

Printed by the Perry Mill Press,
Bromsgrove.

The Railways of Dudley

CONTENTS

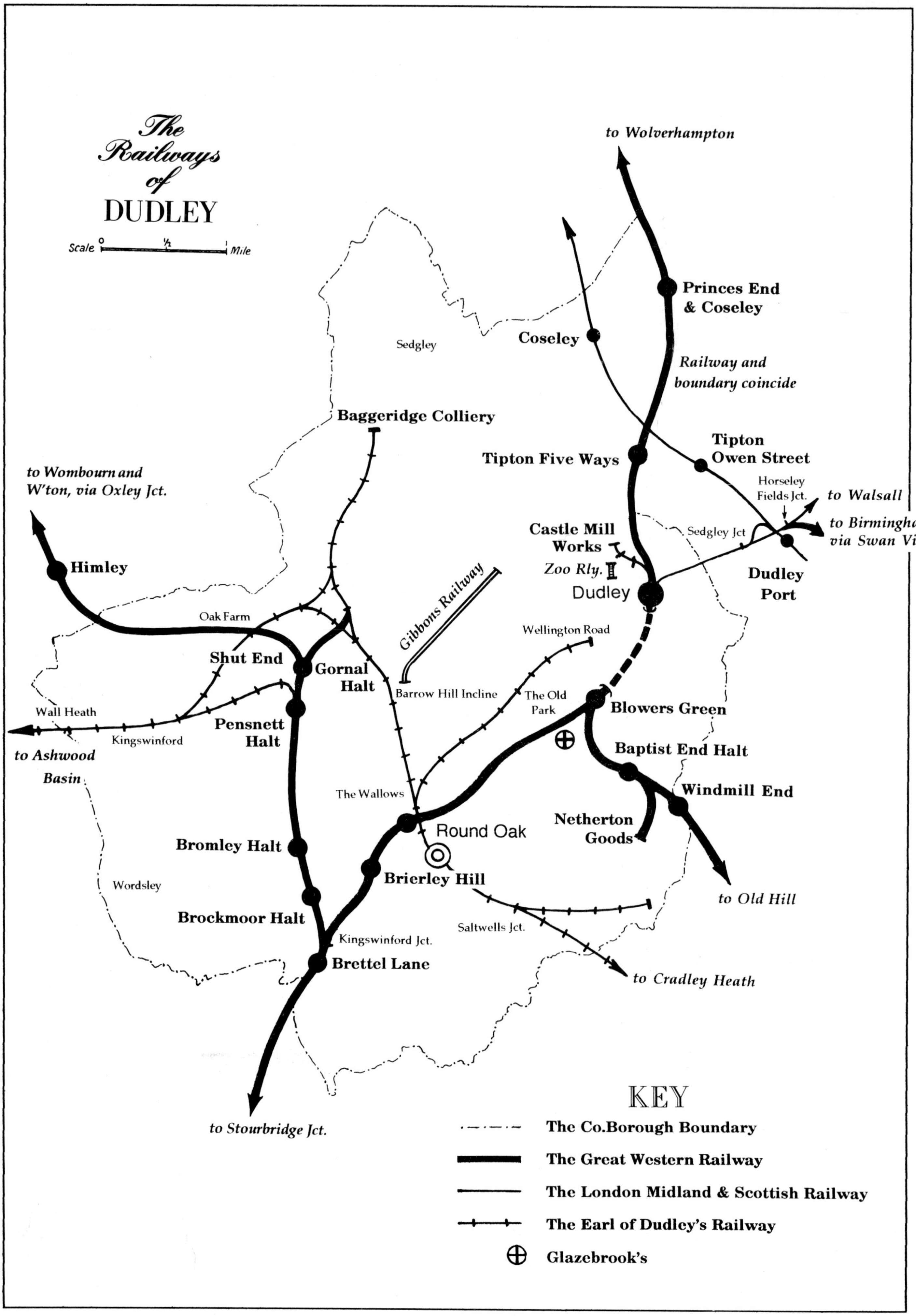
The Railways of DUDLEY
Scale 0 ½ 1 Mile
to Wolverhampton
Princes End & Coseley
Coseley
Railway and boundary coincide
Sedgley
Baggeridge Colliery
Tipton Owen Street
Tipton Five Ways
to Wombourn and W'ton, via Oxley Jct.
Horseley Fields Jct.
to Walsall
to Birmingham via Swan Villag
Sedgley Jct
Castle Mill Works
Zoo Rly.
Dudley
Dudley Port
Himley
Gibbons Railway
Oak Farm
Wellington Road
Shut End
Gornal Halt
Barrow Hill Incline
The Old Park
Blowers Green
Wall Heath
Pensnett Halt
Kingswinford
to Ashwood Basin
Baptist End Halt
Windmill End
The Wallows
Netherton Goods
Round Oak
Bromley Halt
Brierley Hill
Wordsley
to Old Hill
Brockmoor Halt
Saltwells Jct.
Kingswinford Jct.
Brettel Lane
to Cradley Heath
to Stourbridge Jct.
KEY
The Co.Borough Boundary
The Great Western Railway
The London Midland & Scottish Railway
The Earl of Dudley's Railway
Glazebrook's

Introduction

At 12.55.pm., ten minutes late, 0-6-0 PT No. 7418 steamed out of Old Hill on the last regular passenger train to traverse the Bumble Hole line to Dudley, on Saturday 13th June 1964. The service was usually provided by an "auto train", or single coach "push-pull" set, but on this occasion the locomotive supplied by Stourbridge Shed was not equipped for such work, and had to run round its train at Old Hill for the return to Dudley. The other unusual feature of the trip was that the train was crowded. On the previous Saturday only three passengers had joined the train, but on 13th June the single carriage was was full and many of us had to stand in the limited space of the luggage compartment.

It was a typical Black Country adventure: sad, happy, sociable, slightly bizarre, and "never to be repeated". I grabbed some window space from which to record the event with my borrowed cine camera. One or two people had still cameras, but most of us acted like party guests, intoxicated by the pleasures of passing Cox's Lane, Darby End, the mysteries of the canal-dominated landscape of Windmill End, the hills converging around us as we approached Dudley to be swallowed by the tunnel north of Blowers Green, and spat out into Dudley Station.

Only after the party was over, and preserved Prairie tank no.4555 had made its way over the line with a farewell special, did I realise that as party guests we should have swapped addresses and pledged ourselves to the common cause of recording and celebrating the history of Dudley's railways - just in case they should one day cease to exist altogether. (An impossible thought in 1964.) However, the feeling faded and, like almost everybody else, I forgot to take my camera down to Dudley station and record the scene for posterity.

Even while making a cine film early in 1967, and using the demolition of Dudley Station as a backdrop, I failed to appreciate the fact that Dudley's railway "presence" was vanishing and I was not doing much about it. Ironically the cine film I made at the time made much use of the Black Country landscape as a metaphor for "change" and "intimations of mortality". Yet it was not until the 1980s that I really woke up and was struck by the obvious - if the Black Country is really forever vanishing, changing, re-creating itself again, it could be a good idea to make a visual record of that process.

When the "real" Black Country is finally destroyed and replaced by a 21st century suburbia our grandchildren may want to see our pictures of the windmill at Windmill End, the swans at Swan Village, or the green at Blowers Green. Well.... Sorry! I haven't seen such pictures, let alone taken any myself, but here are some pictures of the trains that once enlivened those places.

Dudley's railways were not the most photographed part of Britain's railway system, and anyone setting out to collect pictures for a book such as this soon finds out that it is a much neglected subject. It can only be done by bringing together the talents of a number of photographers and asking them for the odd one or two photographs they may have taken at Dudley. Thank goodness there were a few local enthusiasts around at the end of the 1950s and the beginning of the 1960s who showed more foresight than myself, and we must be particularly grateful that thirty years later these photographers are willing to share these pictures from their archives, and help us re-create a composite picture of Dudley's railways.

It is strange that Dudley's railways have been comparatively neglected for they were not without interest, particularly if we draw a boundary around the County Borough as created in 1966. Within this boundary had once existed a rich mixture of railways, ranging from obscure narrow gauge tramways linking pits and canal wharves, the Earl of Dudley's vast railway system with tentacles stretching in all directions, and a public railway station shared by two main line companies - the GWR and the LMS, later the Western Region and London Midland Region of British Railways.

Even in the 1960s the variety was impressive: steam was being replaced by diesels down at Round Oak, but the NCB remained committed to steam on their line up to Baggeridge Colliery, Dudley Station was served by DMUs, steam push-pull trains and a variety of goods traffic including Palethorpe's sausages and much travelled pigeon baskets. Over the years we have had a railway in Dudley Zoo, and now we are proud possessor of a monorail! We even had a quarter of a mile of railway in the Black Country Museum for a few weeks in 1991.

Dudley no longer has a standard gauge railway north of Round Oak, but within the boundary of the area covered by this book, we were in at the birth of railways - back in 1829 Agenoria had entered traffic on the Earl of Dudley's Shut End Railway - the same year as Rocket won the Rainhill Trials and entered every schoolchild's history of the railways of the World.

One of the main reasons for producing this book in 1994 is that the story of Dudley's railways seemed to come to an end in 1993 when the line through Dudley from Bescot to Round Oak closed. The railway north of Stourbridge Junction still climbs up to Brierley Hill and terminates at Round Oak Rail Terminal, and the branch to Pensnett still exists at the time of writing, but trains no longer trundle over Parkhead Viaduct, plunge into the tunnel beneath Dudley itself or squeal round the curve beneath the Tipton Road. There has been talk of operating a passenger service from Walsall to Dudley once more, and the Midland Metro proposed such a line, and more, in the proposals for a light rail system that might re-invigorate the Black Country, or at least relieve some of the road congestion. If any of these schemes come to fruition they will hardly invalidate our efforts from a 1994 perspective to put Dudley's railways "on the map" in the world of railway literature.

This book could not have been created without the help, which I gratefully acknowledge, of the following people, arranged in alphabetical order:

Geoff Bannister, George Bennett, Donald Bytheway, Lawrence Brownhill, W.A.Camwell, Roger Carpenter, Dr. Paul Collins, Roger Crombleholme, Tony Cooke, Fay Davis, John Dew, Paul Dorney, John Harris, Ron Hartshorne, Nigel Hazlewood, Lens of Sutton, Michael Mensing, Viv Morgan, Gordon Nutt, Jack Reynolds, Brian Robbins, Eric Rogers, Edgar Rumble, Jessie Sambrook, Rob Selvey, Martin Shenton, Peter Shoesmith, Hugh Sykes, Richard Taylor, Kenneth Tibbetts, Stan Webb, John Williams, and Dudley Library's Local History Centre. I wish to thank Michael Hale for some advice, and Philip Barnard for his proof reading.

Many writers have contributed to our collective knowledge of Dudley's railways over the years that have elapsed since C.R.Clinker set out the outlines with his Midlands Chronology. On the lesser known world of Dudley's "other railways" we owe a great debt to Messrs Hoskison and Gale for their work on the Pensnett Railway, and more recently to Ray Shill for his magnificent West Midlands Industrial Locomotive Handbook.

As one who "arrived too late", missed many an opportunity, but lived to try and make amends, I must take responsibility for any errors that exist in this book.

Ned Williams
Summer 1994.

GREAT WESTERN RAILWAY.

JUBILEE EXHIBITION
OF
HISTORICAL OBJECTS,
Industries and Fine Arts,
AT
DUDLEY

Commencing Saturday, June 25th, Monday, June 27th, & Wednesday, June 29th,

CHEAP TICKETS
WILL BE ISSUED TO

DUDLEY

EVERY MONDAY, WEDNESDAY, AND SATURDAY,

Until further Notice, as under—

FROM	AT			Fares there and back, Third Class (including admission to the Exhibition). Adults.		Children.	
	P.M.	P.M.	P.M.	s.	d.	s.	d.
Worcester (Shrub Hill)	12 50	2 5	3 40	4	7	2	6½
Fernhill Heath	12 57	—	—	4	2	2	4
Droitwich	1 5	2 17	3 50	3	8	2	1
Hartlebury	1 20	2 31	—	2	9	1	7½
Newnham Bridge	12 14	—	—	4	8	2	7
Neen Sollars	12 21	—	—	4	3	2	4½
Cleobury Mortimer	12 32	—	—	3	8	2	1
Wyre Forest	12 39	—	—	3	5	1	11½
Bewdley	12 55	—	—	2	8	1	7
Kidderminster	1 30	2 41	3 50	2	1	1	3½
Churchill	1 37	2 48	3 56	1	7	1	0½
Hagley	1 45	2 55	4 4	1	4	0	11
Stourbridge Junction	1 55	3 7	4 35	1	3	0	10½
Lye	2 54	4 14	6 19	1	5	0	11½
Cradley	2 49	4 9	6 14	1	3	0	10½
Halesowen	—	3 18	6 38	1	3	0	10½
Wellington	—	2 28	—	4	3	2	4½
Oakengates	—	2 37	—	3	9	2	1½
Shifnal	—	2 47	—	3	0	1	9
Albrighton	—	2 45	—	2	2	1	4
Codsall	—	2 54	—	1	9	1	1½
Hatton	—	1 43	—	4	2	2	4
Kingswood	—	1 50	—	3	6	2	0
Knowle	—	1 55	3 25	2	10	1	8
Solihull	—	2 10	3 32	2	5	1	5½
Olton	—	2 15	3 37	2	2	1	4
Acocks Green	—	2 19	3 40	2	0	1	3
Small Heath	—	2 25	3 46	1	8	1	2
Bordesley	—	2 31	3 51	1	6	1	0
Birmingham	1 10	3 0	5 0	1	6	1	0
Hockley	1 14	3 4	5 4	1	4	0	11
Soho	1 17	—	—	1	3	0	10½
Handsworth	1 21	3 9	5 9	1	3	0	10½

Passengers return the same day by any Ordinary Train by which they can get to their destination.

The Tickets are not transferable, are available on the day of issue only, and by the Trains shown above. Passengers using them by any other Train, or between any other Stations, will be charged the full Ordinary Fare. Tickets and Bills may be obtained at the Stations.

PADDINGTON, *May*, 1887. **J. GRIERSON,** *General Manager.*

(B.D. 167) Martin Billing, Son, and Co., Printers, Livery Street, Birmingham.

GWR DUDLEY ZOO

MONDAY, AUGUST 7th

BOOKINGS

– TO –

DUDLEY

(ZOO ADJOINS THE STATION)

FROM	Depart		RETURN FARES Third Class		Arrival on Return
	a.m.	p.m.	s.	d.	p.m.
SHIRLEY	10A 44	2 12	2	1	7 58
YARDLEY WOOD	10A 48	2 15	2	0	7 54
HALL GREEN	10A 52	2 18	1	10	7 48
DUDLEY .. .. arrive	11 40	3 20	A—Change at Birmingham (Snow Hill) and proceed at 11.20 a.m.		

RETURN SAME DAY FROM DUDLEY at 6.55 p.m.

DUDLEY ZOO

The setting is unique ; an Ancient Castle full of interest in itself and representing stage by stage the history of our country ; a wooded hillside on which the Castle stands adapted by experienced Architects so that the animals which are housed in the Zoological Gardens can be seen to the best advantage in beautiful modern settings which in no way spoil or interfere with the charm of the great Castle itself.

The Castle Moat has been used for Beavers, Pelicans, Flamingoes, Sea-Lions, etc.

To quote only a few of the animals, etc., to be seen, are the following :—

LIONS	TIGERS	POLAR BEARS	BABOONS
MONKEYS	KINKAJOUS	BLACKBUCKS	LLAMAS
RHEAS	CAMEL	ZEBRAS	BISONS
ELEPHANTS	EMUS	BROWN BEARS	VULTURES
OWLS	WOLVES	FOXES	DINGOES

The Bird House—full of Birds of all kinds and the Penguin Pool should not be missed. Elephant and Pony Riding takes place during the Season.

The Children's Corner is full of interest. Finest Bear Pit in the World.

SEE THE FAMOUS CASTLE RUINS

ADMISSION CHARGES—ADULTS 1/- CHILDREN 6d.

NOTICE AS TO CONDITIONS.—These tickets are issued subject to the Notices and Conditions shown in the Company's current Time Tables. For LUGGAGE ALLOWANCES also see Time Tables.

Children under Three years of age, Free ; Three and under Fourteen, Half-price.

TICKETS ISSUED AND DATED IN ADVANCE AT STATIONS AND OFFICES.

For any further information respecting the arrangements shown in this Bill, application should be made at any of the Offices, Agencies, or to
W. E. HART, Divisional Superintendent, Snow Hill Station, Birmingham. *Telephone Central 5071 (extension "Enquiries")*,
or to
F. R. POTTER, Superintendent of the Line, Paddington Station, W.

Paddington Station, July, 1939. **JAMES MILNE, General Manager.**

B.H. 31/624. B.H. 3,000 Printed in Great Britain by Joseph Wones Ltd., West Bromwich ; also Birmingham and London.

Dudley Station - Historical Background

Dudley stands on the ridge that separates the two halves of the Black Country. Standing at the top of the Castle's keep it is possible to gaze eastwards across Tipton, Wednesbury, out towards Walsall, over to the rising ground at Bar Beacon, and southwards to the outline of the centre of Birmingham. Maybe somewhere over the eastern horizon are the Urals. To the West, although not visible at that point, is the half of the Black Country that stretches out through Brierley Hill, followed by the countryside of Staffordshire, Shropshire and beyond into Wales. At the foot of Castle Hill once stood Dudley's railway station and a cluster of lines that once took passengers and goods to the places seen from the top of the hill.

But towns on the crests of ridges are not easily reached by rail, and present something of a crisis to the railway builder - anxious to find a level and accessible route for his line, while at the same time wanting to serve the needs of communities and industries that will bring his line its profit and justify his investment. Two early chapters in railway history illustrate the fact that the town of Dudley was not going to be first on the railway map. In June 1829 the "Agenoria" steamed along the Shutt End Railway a few miles west of Dudley, providing part of the railway journey made by the coal from the collieries in the Pensnett area westwards to the Staffordshire and Worcestershire Canal at Ashwood. Canals seemed destined to be the national carrier of heavy goods that would link pits and furnaces to ports and far-off cities.

By 1837 it looked as if the railway might challenge the canals, and railway technology had reached the point where lines were being planned on an "inter-city" scale. It was conceivable that the rails might extend from the capital to the Mersey. In July 1837 the Grand Junction Railway, as part of such a link, opened from Birmingham to Warrington, where it met the Liverpool & Manchester Railway. The line skirted the eastern flank of the Black Country, about five miles away from Dudley.

Thus it was that Dudley, in the heart of that grimy miracle called The Black Country, was not on anyone's map as the first railways were planned. However, just as the canal had eventually approached Dudley, and burrowed beneath the ridge, it was inevitable that before long railways would overcome geographical difficulties and would put the town on the map.

Railway planners and builders started putting Dudley on their maps in the 1840s. The Oxford Worcester & Wolverhampton Railway (OWWR) was authorised in August 1845. Linking the towns in its name, the railway was to approach the Black Country from the south west , entering the industrial area near Stourbridge, and climbing steadily up through Brierley Hill and thence to Dudley, via a tunnel beneath the ridge, and then on to Wolverhampton. On 3rd August 1846 two other railways gained parliamentary and royal approval to put Dudley on their maps. These were the South Staffordshire Railway (SSR) which was to leave the Midland Railway at Wychnor Junction and head towards Dudley via Walsall, and the Birmingham Wolverhampton & Dudley Railway (BW&D) which was to build a line from Birmingham Snow Hill to Priestfield just outside Wolverhampton with a branch from Swan Village round to Dudley. The SSR had the backing of the Midland Railway, and the BW&D was an extension of the Great Western Railway which was making its way from London up to Birmingham and with its sights set on reaching the southern shore of the Mersey.

None of these plans pleased the London & North Western Railway (LNWR) which had been formed on 1st January 1846 by an amalgamation of the Grand Junction Railway, the London & Birmingham Railway, and the Manchester & Birmingham Railway. The LNWR was keen to reach the industrial areas around Wednesbury and Dudley, and therefore promoted its own Birmingham, Wolverhampton & Stour Valley Railway (hereafter called the Stour Valley Railway), which was also authorised on the same day. The Stour Valley line was to link Birmingham with Wolverhampton, with a branch from Oldbury to Dudley.

Another complication at the time was that the SSR and Stour Valley Railway were to be built to standard gauge, but the BW&D was to be built to the GWR's broad gauge with a third rail providing mixed gauge facilities. The OWWR changed sides and allegiances but had been authorised to bring standard gauge tracks to Dudley. Dudley seemed to be one of those places where the gauge war would become a reality if the BW&D brought their mixed gauge line into the station and this prospect stimulated the SSR to "get there first".

During 1849 the SSR sought to make agreement with the OWWR concerning a joint station at Dudley and took the precaution of making sure it acquired enough land to provide its own station should the joint one not materialise

The first train to reach Dudley was on the standard gauge SSR line on 1st November 1849 although, at the time, the line was still not completed. This was run for the benefit of the company's directors, and had a train not been run by that date, the BW&D would have exploited its right to build a mixed gauge line into Dudley. A month later the directors expressed their wish that the line to Dudley be open by mid January 1850. Perhaps this impatience is reflected in the fact that the line opened with limited provision for goods traffic, and "temporary facilities for passengers".

The South Staffordshire Railway's line opened to Dudley on 1st March 1850 for goods traffic, possibly for only conveying its own goods traffic needed to complete its work on the line. A few days later the company held its half-yearly meeting at the George Hotel in Walsall, with Mr.Forster in the chair. He was able to tell the shareholders present that the engineer had reported that the "whole of the main line was now open for goods traffic".

The meeting was reported in detail in the Wolverhampton Chronicle and the story is mainly concerned with the finances of the company. However, it does tell us that the directors were still impatient to open their new line to Dudley for passenger traffic, but the engineer thought the line should be given time to settle particularly where it passed over coal workings. Mr.Forster told everyone he was looking forward to a *"free and unbroken railway journey between Dudley and Birmingham"*, and, in the light of local dissatisfaction felt by Dudley folk about their station in later years, he made the interesting statement: *"Satisfactory arrangements have also been made with the Oxford Worcester & Wolverhampton Railway for the formation of a joint station at Dudley highly advantageous for the traffic of that town and the neighbourhood."*

Two months later, on Wednesday 1st May 1850, the SSR's line to Dudley was formally opened for passengers, goods and parcels traffic. The event was reported in the Wolverhampton Chronicle:

"In honour of the opening the stations along the line were gaily and tastefully decorated with evergreens and great numbers of flags and banners, and locomotive engines were in their holiday attire - appropriate devices were hung from every available point.

The first trains started at about half past eight o'clock and throughout the day large crowds lined almost every bridge and embankment, testifying their hearty pleasure such an event had universally excited. As train after train swept past the great ironworks that lie so thickly between Wednesbury, Great Bridge and Dudley Port, the grim forms of men were seen issuing forth to greet the mighty Promethean spirit whose iron sinews they had perhaps helped to fashion.

The great incident of the day, however, took place at Dudley about four o'clock in the afternoon. The inhabitants had been requested to accompany the directors in procession from the station to the town, and at the hour mentioned there could not have been fewer that 20,000 persons gathered together from Dudley and the immediate district....

On the platform were the most respectable of inhabitants, with many gentlemen connected with the iron trade, and the boys of the Grammar School were marshalled in front, under Rev. A. K. Thompson, head master, and Rev. J.F.Fairhead, second master."

The directors of the SSR arrived into this scene by train, having set out from Walsall, and as soon as they arrived the Chairman, Mr.Forster, was presented with an address written in Latin by the Grammer School headmaster, and delivered by Thomas Auden, the Senior Boy! Mr.Forster accepted this gracefully, and responded by offering the entire school a free train trip to Lichfield the following week. He also urged the boys to visit the local caverns which were about to be illuminated and opened to the public.

The procession then set off for the town, led by the Mayor of Dudley, Thomas Fereday, and the town's brass band. One hundred and twenty guests then sat down to dinner at 5.00.pm, followed by countless toasts and speeches.

The Latin ode written by the headmaster became the subject of a local legend in which the engine driver is asked his opinion of the text - but apparently neither the driver nor the fireman could produce a satisfactory opinion. The local newspaper later published a translation in case its own readers struggled with Latin.

Below: The general view of Dudley Station from the top of Station Drive around the turn of the century. An "up" GWR train pauses at Platform 2 on its way south. Note that Dudley South Signal Box can be seen without its brick skirt, and the LNWR no.2 Signal Box can be seen at the southern end of their platform. On the extreme right hand edge of the picture it is just possible to see the LNWR engine shed.
(Photo: Lens of Sutton)

The newspaper announced the commencement of a service from Dudley to the Midland Railway at Alrewas, but the services that were inaugurated on the new line made a little more sense than that suggests. The SSR provided six services a day to and from Birmingham via Bescot Junction, taking 40 minutes for the journey, three further trains each way between Dudley and Walsall without a Birmingham connection, and a further three each way that proceeded out to Alrewas and to Burton on Trent. As can be seen from the poster, it was even suggested that the service linked Dudley with Wolverhampton, by taking the train to Walsall and catching the connecting coach service!

The SSR were keen to stimulate traffic and were keen to see Castle Hill developed as leisure traffic destination. The limestone caverns beneath the hill were "illuminated" for the first time during that year as forecast on 1st May by Mr.Forster. The station was better located for access to Castle Hill than it was for access to the town.

One problem concerning the SSR's terminus at Dudley was that access to and from the station was via a length of single track, and this resulted in collisions in October 1854 and May 1855.

Over the years the station facilities at Dudley came in for continual criticism, but of course both the SSR and the OWWR opened to "temporary" stations, and with hindsight it appears that things improved steadily. (See G.P.Neele's comments below.) A December 1850 inventory of SSR fixtures reveals that the company had the following facilities available at Dudley: a passenger platform and a goods platform, a booking office, waiting room, lamp room, pointsman's wooden "box", a separate goods station, agent's office and delivery office.

In the following year, 1851, the SSR obtained powers to build a spur from Sedgeley Junction to the Stour Valley Railway's proposed station at Dudley Port. The latter opened as a station on the Stour Valley line on 1st July 1852. The Sedgeley Junction - Dudley Port spur was opened on 1st January 1854, and the LNWR had running powers over this line into Dudley.

The OWWR tackled some work at Dudley in 1846, but generally the years that followed its 1845 authorisation passed slowly in terms of progress in building the line. The Dudley contract was taken up by Buxton & Clark of Sheffield, and the work was expected to take up to three years. It was reckoned that seven million bricks would go into lining the Dudley tunnel, and that five shafts from the surface would have to be sunk to make the tunnelling possible. Some of the waste material from the tunnel was tipped onto mounds at the northern end, creating the "White Nobs" that then became the patch regularly used by the fair whenever showmen came to Dudley. Access was from Trindle Road and the terrain was far from flat but it played a significant part in local fairground history!

The bridge carrying the Dudley-Birmingham Turnpike road over the OWWR between the tunnel and the station also gave the builders some problems to face. The arch of the bridge was built while the cutting beneath was still filled with earth. The earth was then removed and, in May 1847, the centre of the bridge collapsed. The matter was

reported in the Worcester Chronicle of 20th May 1847:

The portion that has given way is about two yards in depth, and about five yards in length.... The damage already done is very considerable; many say that it will take at least £1000 to repair it, and others say that the bridge, to be considered safe will have to be entirely rebuilt. It is said that the cause of the accident is mainly attributed to to the earth being removed from the middle of the arch first, instead of being removed from under the sides first... Be that as it may, the whole expense will have to fall upon the company, their engineer having certified the work to be complete. The accident is much to be regretted as the bridge was a very fine piece of work, and an ornament to that part of the town, the span of the arch being about 73 feet.

We understand that the whole of the shafts of the tunnel are standing unworked in consequence of the navvies having struck for a rise of wages.

While the SSR line was being brought into full use in May 1850, the OWWR directors, down in London, were still discussing their intentions of making contact with the SSR at Dudley. Mr.Rufford told a meeting at that time that scarcely anything had been done on the five mile stretch from Dudley to Wolverhampton.

The section extending the OWWR from Stourbridge to Dudley was opened on 16th November 1852 to goods traffic, and for passenger traffic on 20th December. Once again a "temporary station" was brought into use, and for a number of years the inhabitants of Dudley had to put up with the two "temporary stations" (the SSR's and the OWWR's), however inadequate.

With the line open to Dudley, the OWWR once again looked into the matter of providing a joint station and the problems of exchanging traffic. As late as September 1853 the OWWR 's Land & Works Committee was still looking into this matter, suggesting that the two companies served Dudley "separately" for quite some time.

In 1853 the OWWR extended northwards from Dudley towards Tipton, and on the 1st December opened a junction with the Stour Valley line via what was known as the Tipton Curve. The following year the OWWR made its way into Wolverhampton via its own line through Daisy Bank, Bilston and Priestfield, where it was soon to be joined by the mixed gauge BW&D, which by then had become fully vested in the GWR . At Wolverhampton the OWWR shared the Low Level station with the BW&D, and the OWWR itself continued northwards to a junction with the Grand Junction line at Bushbury. Despite laying mixed gauge track, the OWWR line through Dudley was principally operated as a standard gauge line. (The General Traffic & Works Committee of the OWWR read a letter from Mr.Fowler, the engineer, in April 1854 reporting that he had passed an engine and carriages over the down line, on the broad gauge rails, from Wolvercote to Wolverhampton.) The GWR line from Birmingham to Wolverhampton was operated as a broad gauge line.

On 1st July 1860 the OWWR line through Dudley became part of the West Midl and Railway, and as from 1st August 1863 the West Midlands Railway amalgamated with the Great Western Railway. Meanwhile the WMR had carried out some work first mooted by the OWWR to open a line from Dudley into the area immediately south west of the ridge. Thus the WMR had obtained authorisation on 17th July 1862 for a line from Netherton (Blowers Green) to Old Hill and on to Halesowen, with branches to canal basins at Netherton and Halesowen. The line was difficult to build as it was much undermined by the extraction of coal, and it did not open from Dudley to Halesowen, via Old Hill, until 1st March 1878. At Old Hill it crossed the Stourbridge Extension Railway making its way from Stourbridge Junction to Galton Junction and Handsworth Junction. This line was always the GWR's "Birmingham Branch" and the OWWR line through Dudley remained the "main line".

Another part of the pattern of train services to and from Dudley was made possible on 1st September 1866 when the line from the BW&D/GWR's station at Swan Village was opened to Horsley Fields Junction of the SSR line near Dudley Port. This made possible a "direct" GWR service from Dudley to Birmingham Snow Hill. It had been authorised by a GWR Act of 13th July 1863 and planned as a standard gauge line, unlike the BW&D's plans of 1846 which would have brought the broad gauge to Dudley from this direction. The GWR trains running over LNWR track between Dudley and the junction at Horsley Fields did not call at the LNWR's station at Dudley Port Low Level, and at Dudley itself they had run right past the LNWR platform and then reverse into the GWR platform, until agreement was eventually reached that they could use the LNWR platform.

Below: GWR 0-6-0ST no.1513 at Dudley, In the background is the outline of the LNWR engine shed and a LNWR coach. Above the retaining wall it is possible to see two tramcars of the Dudley, Stourbridge & District Tramways Co. in the siding in the narrow strip between the wall and the tram depot. (About 1903)
(Photo: Collection of Roger Carpenter)

There was further excitement in 1866 when the GWR announced its intention of finding a location for a carriage works. Dudley was one of a number of possible sites. In February 1866 a meeting of the town council elected representatives to form a deputation to meet the GWR in March - but the GWR decided that Dudley was not to be chosen.

The SSR was absorbed by the London & North Western Railway in 1867, having been leased to the LNWR since 1861, thus, by the end of the 1860s, the GWR and LNWR shared the honour of serving Dudley. Now in the hands of two large companies there was a chance that Dudley station might enjoy some of the improvements that had been awaited by the local community. As early as June 1857 there had been "an important and influential Public Meeting" at the old Town Hall, under the chairmanship of the Mayor, John Renaud Esq., at which the railway companies were identified as failing to provide satisfactory accommodation for the general public at Dudley station. (See comment on these facilities below)

Although Dudley escaped involvement in the gauge war, it had materialised as a "frontier" station between two major railway companies, and the station developed as if it was two separate stations built alongside each other, and each company built its own separate goods facilities, sidings and operational facilities. Life at Dudley Station was also made more interesting by the Midland Railway exercising its right to reach Dudley via the South Staffordshire line, at least for goods traffic.

****

The development of facilities at Dudley.

When the OWWR was pushed through to Wolverhampton in 1854, an engine shed was built at Dudley, and this remained in use until 1870 when it was made redundant by the opening of a new GWR shed near Stourbridge Junction, although the engine turntable appears to have remained in situ for a long time after. The OWWR engine shed is thought to have been a long wooden two-road structure. Undated plans in the Public Record Office describe how it was to be rebuilt into a grain warehouse, but it appears that nothing came of such plans. Instead it seems to have been removed altogether and the site was used by the wooden goods shed seen in the photograph on page 24. (One "legend" suggests that it was removed from Dudley and re-erected at Stourbridge, which is theoretically possible at it appears to have been built in wooden sections.)

The SSR's original facilities at Dudley, or the lack of them, became legendary, consisting of a few temporary shed-like structures and a single platform. The LNWR gradually improved matters and expanded facilities. During the "Maclean era" (June 1850 - January 1861) Walsall had been the SSR's centre of operations, and Dudley was an "outpost", but the LNW R saw the need for engine stabling facilities at Dudley, and a shed was eventually built in the shadow of the retaining wall between the Tipton Road and the southern end of the station. It was a sub-shed of Walsall and by the 1920s only a single engine was stabled there. By the end of the 1930s it was no longer in use, and the sidings on the site simply became carriage accommodation.

The railway companies also built separate good facilities at Dudley, as well as providing marshalling yards for the exchange of goods wagons. The GWR yard in the shadow of Castle Hill was provided with a three road goods shed on the site of the former engine shed (See above). The LNWR built a goods shed on the far side of the Tipton Road, and the Midland Railway was also provided with a small shed.

The rail access to the LNWR goods facilities on the far side of Tipton Road was via a separate bridge and the timber building must have adjoined the brick structure that still exists today. (see pictures on pages 24 and 39). Later the LNWR built a large shed and bonded store on the station side of the Tipton road, in the "V" formed by the divergence of the GWR and LNWR lines north of Dudley. This brick built building, often seen in views looking north from Dudley station platforms, was probably built in the 1880s. LNWR plans of October 1881 survive in the PRO relating to the provision of stables to be built along the northern perimeter of the yard that accommodated the new goods shed. The stables included stalls for Pickford's horses as well as the LNWR's own horses, and greatly extended a building that had previously accommodated a few LNWR horses and a few Shropshire Union horses. The stables were probably built 1882/3.

Access by road to the goods facilities at Dudley was entirely separate and remote - the GWR being reached via Station Drive, the LNWR (and Midland) facilities being reached via both sides of Tipton Road. In BR days this was the reason for having to distinguish the facilities by name rather than by company, and the names Dudley Castle and Dudley Town were adopted.

For many years Dudley Station was administered as two stations, and therefore there was a GWR Station Master and a LNWR one, but there were three Goods Agents as the Midland Railway was also part of the goods "scene". At the Station Drive entrance to the passenger station each company had its own separate booking office window, but closer working arrangements between the two companies eventually prevailed. (See Kenneth Tibbett's account of working at Dudley.)

When we come across nineteenth century accounts of the "disgraceful facilities" provided for passengers at Dudley, it is tempting to think that the station that we knew at the end of passenger services in the 1960s was very different to what may have existed a century earlier. This does not seem to have been entirely so! The basic provision of two island platforms each used by the separate companies, linked by a long footbridge running from Station Drive across the entire station layout to Tipton Road, and with stairs down to each platform seems to have materialised by the late 1850s. This is made quite clear in a letter of complaint written by Mr.C.F.G.Clark in October 1857. Mr.Clark was a prominent local citizen, who became Dudley's Mayor in 1861. He collected all sorts of documents that he felt would relate to the future understanding of Dudley's history, and published these in 1881 in his book, "Curiosities of Dudley and the Black Country". He included his own letter to the Midland Counties Express, and it is worth quoting from some of its lengthy, but elegant, text. He was at the Town Hall meeting of June 1857 mentioned above and was generally complaining about lack of response by the railway companies despite their promises.

"If the aged, lame, infirm, or timid railway traveller casts his anxious eye towards the Dudley station, expecting to find an improvement effected at that delightful arena of decorum and propriety, more especially on a wet Saturday night, he will be most woefully deceived. For can it be supposed, Mr. Editor, that a railway company, already prolific in blunders, misunderstandings, and broken promises, could be so egregariously foolish as recently to remove their ticket office at the Dudley Station from its legitimate ground floor platform to the extreme entrance of that highly artistic wooden tunnel, spanning its unwieldly proportions across the domain of two important railway companies! To passengers starting from Dudley the boon is offered, we presume, as being highly convenient to take your ticket before taking your choice of standing upon that spacious gallery....

To the casual traveller who may be so unlucky as to require re-booking from an incoming train on the South Staffordshire line, the amount of annoyance and physical exertion cannot fail to be intolerable.... ....arriving by a late train on the South Stafford line, and having to hobble or rush up and down two pairs of slippery stairs, then along that precious gangway, for another ticket, occupying some considerable time at the present spacious ticket office, ere they can arrive at the object of their solicitude, the waiting train below."

Clark's letter of October 1857 also expressed fury about the rumours that the OWWR were going to improve station facilities south of Dudley before improving Dudley itself. However Netherton station did not undergo substantial change until replaced by the new Dudley (South Side) & Netherton in 1878. The station at Woodside did not materialise until 1895, and then only lasted until 1st January 1917.

The key to improving Dudley Station seemed to be co-operation between the various interested parties. A meeting was held on 16th July 1858 that seemed to secure this co-operation, and everyone agreed to accept the decisions of an independent arbiter. The meeting included Mr.Moon, a director of the LNWR, R.C. Chawnor, chairman of the SSR, Mr.Fenton, chairman of the OWWR, plus Lord Alfred Paget, Mr.McClean, the lessee of the SSR, and Richard Smith - the

Earl of Dudley's agent. The Wolverhampton Chronicle declared: *"We are happy to inform our readres that there is at length the prospect of the town being accommodated with a station commensurate with the importance of the place, and adequate for the great amount of business transacted at it."* However, it seems that the station carried on developing in the form that had already evolved.

The two companies had their own separate signal boxes for controlling trains in their own sections of the station. The GWR had a South Box at the southern end of their passenger platform, and a North Box strategically placed in the midst of the goods facilities to the north of the station and controlling the line to and from Wolverhampton. The LNWR may have had three boxes in the 1880s, but rationalised this to two: a No.1 at the Tipton Road Bridge end of their station, and a No.2 at the other end. At the beginning of 1935 the No.2 Box was closed and the No.1 became known as Dudley East.

Naturally problems arose out of the situation in which each company had its own method of controlling train movements, and the signal boxes lacked common means of communication. For example, there was an accident on 30th October 1898 when the 11.25.pm GWR train from Birmingham, via Swan Village, ran into a LNWR train standing at the platform. Luckily the latter had emptied itself of passengers but the locomotive was still on the front of the train when the GWR locomotive ploughed into the rear coach. Lt.Col. H.A. Yorke's report blamed the lack of block working between the two company's signal boxes - the GWR were not informed of the arrival of LNWR trains, and the arrival of the GWR's own trains over the LNWR tracks was only signalled by the means of a bell, without the visible information afforded by block instruments.

****

G.P.Neeles's Memories

In 1904 G.P.Neele published his "Railway Reminiscences", reprinted in 1974. In his chapter dealing with the period from 1849 to 1853, he makes a number of comments on the coming of the railways to Dudley. He confirms that the opening of the SSR in May 1850 was seen as a way of linking Dudley to Birmingham by rail and that for a short while through carriages from Dudley were joined to the Walsall-Birmingham trains at Bescot Junction. The opening of the Stour Valley line and the BW&D line later gave much more direct access from the Black Country to the heart of Birmingham. The SSR also took advantage of the OWWR's slow progress in reaching Dudley, and in the early years coach services brought passengers to the SSR railhead at Dudley form Kidderminster, Stourbridge and Brierley Hill.

Mr.Neele also reveals that the SSR very nearly obtained their own lease on Castle Hill, which they hoped to develop as a tourist destination for the line's passengers, but the local council just managed to put a stop to their plans.

Mr. Neele also gives his own brief account, from an SSR point of view, of the development of Dudley Station - seeing it in three distinct phases. First there was the temporary terminus of 1850, followed by the second one built adjacent to the OWWR temporary station. These two temporary stations coexisted for a few years in the 1850s much to the dissatisfaction of Dudley people - but were destroyed by a fire - which led to the new "joint station", which still came in for criticism (see above" until through booking made it a little easier to use.

****

A last attempt to improve Dudley Station?

At the time that Dudley Zoo was opened - in May 1937 - the Council was looking at the whole question of improving the Castle Hill approach to the town. The entrance to the zoo was not the only new development on Castle Hill: The new "Opera House" was under construction replacing the building destroyed by fire the previous year. (By the time it was completed the name "Hippodrome" was used instead of "Opera House".) Next door, the same architect had been responsible for designing the new Plaza Cinema that had opened in May 1936 and had miraculously escaped the fire! On the opposite side of the road a magnificent Odeon was under construction - to be opened in the July of 1937. The Council sent representatives to Paddington to discuss a new improved entrance to Dudley station - hoping that it might be accommodated on the widened overbridge at the foot of the hill. The GWR was "sympathetic" but presumably it was not practical as the platforms were some way from the bridge, and therefore access to and from the station continued to be via Station Drive.

****

Dudley Station since the War

Kenneth Tibbetts' description of his short career in the Booking Office at Dudley station from 1938 to 1941 is a reminder that the station was a busy one, and presumably no one up until that time doubted its future. It is true that the Black Country had already lost some of its rail services and that public transport on the roads had undergone few a revolutions. It must have already been apparent that the rail network of the Black Country did not support a commuter operation found in other urban areas with a similar population, but few would have imagined that the railway would ever cease to serve a town like Dudley.

As from 1st January 1948 the railways of Britain became "British Railways", and many believed a new "rationalised" railway system, maybe even a completely integrated national public transport "system", would evolve. Looking back it seems strange that the new order began by rigorously maintaining the status quo - by organising "regions" within the boundaries of the old companies. Dudley was just the place to see this in operation. Having been served by the GWR and LMS since the previous railway reorganisation of 1923, the railway at Dudley now found it self divided between the Western and Midland Regions of British Railways.

Rationalisation took the form of renaming various stations, not re-allocating them to sensibly defined regions. At Dudley this led to the station's goods facilities being given two names. As from 19th July 1950 the Western Region's goods facilities became "Dudley Castle", and the Midland Region's facilities became "Dudley Town". And just to confuse everyone the Western Region service to Birmingham via Swan Village still had to arrive and depart via the other region's station!

What mattered more was that passenger traffic on all Dudley's rail services was declining throughout the post-war period, and, by the 1960s it was going to become

Left: Great Western days at Dudley - a "Prairie" stands on an "up" train at Platform 2, while a "Pannier" and auto - trailer no.45 stands in the bay. (The "Platform 3" sign appears to be fixed to the station name board.)
(Photo: Lens of Sutton)

inevitable that the survival of such services would be seriously threatened. The first service to be withdrawn did not even survive long enough to be dieselised, and this was the service on the ex OWWR, or "West Midland" line between Wolverhampton and Stourbridge Junction. The service ceased as from 30th July 1962, the last trains therefore running on Sunday 29th July, and within a year the line, which now carried goods-traffic only, was taken from the Western Region and absorbed into a re-defined Midland Region. Although such rationalisation now seems good sense, it is difficult to imagine just how strong old company loyalties could be. Black Country railwaymen whose loyalty was to the GWR, and the Western Region", felt this was just "another nail in the coffin".

The Midland Region, or "London Midland Region" to give its correct title, maintained the surviving rail services to Dudley for a year or two longer, and most of these services were diesel-operated. These services finally ceased as a result of the fall of the "Beeching Axe" - Dr.Beeching's plan to close unremunerative lines, "to make the railways pay", and to re-shape the system.

On Saturday 13th June 1964, the service between Dudley and Old Hill witnessed the passing of the last train. Whatever outcry we like to think was made about closing such services, so few people turned up to see the last train run that the one-coach train could carry them all. It is true that the single coach was packed, but regular passengers could be counted on the fingers of one hand. It had the dignity of being a steam train hauled by an exGWR pannier tank, but with hindsight perhaps even that was a symbol of how anachronistic the service had become. The ex GWR service to Birmingham, via Swan Village, ran for the last time on the following day, and seemed to excite even less interest as the train was a diesel multiple unit.

The last regular passenger service to and from Dudley was on the South Staffordshire line between Dudley and Walsall. This closed to passengers on 6th July 1964, and was a DMU operated service at the time of closure. Within two years Dudley had lost all its passenger services. Parcels traffic continued to be handled at the station for a while, until that was transferred to the exLMS goods shed. Goods traffic continued to arrive and depart from Dudley until August 1966.

Meanwhile other developments were taking place. Dr.Beeching, although remembered for axing unremunerative passenger services, approved of goods traffic being carried by rail providing it was done in a modern and cost effective manner. Ideally the railways were looking for customers who could be served by containers - brought to the railhead by road, transferred to permanently assembled rakes of container-bearing wagons and moved to their destination by the trainload - not marshalled and re-marshalled into endless short trips made by local goods trains serving a host of sidings and yards.

This page from a pre-war Dudley Almanac featured three views of Dudley Station: 1. A GWR "pannier" waits at the signal on platform 2 with an up train to Stourbridge Junction. 2. A view across the station footbridge looking through the booking hall towards the Tipton Road.

3. A view looking up Station drive towards the foot of Castle Hill and the Station Hotel. Beneath the canopy one of Bantock's lorries working for the GWR Express Parcels Service has backed up to the station entrance.

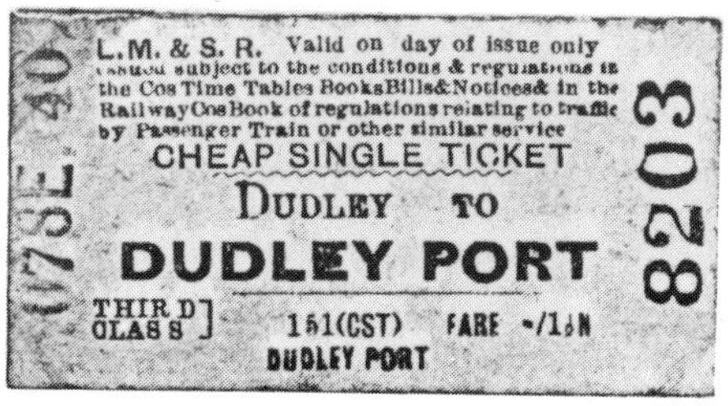

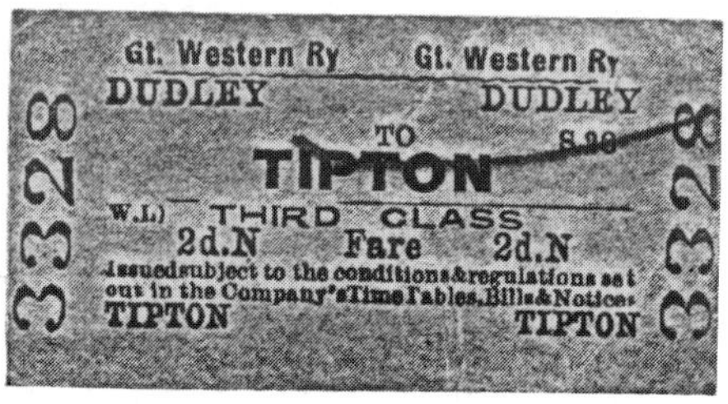

It was announced that the Black Country was to have a brand new Freightliner Depot and that it would be built on the site of Dudley Station and the exGWR part of the railway.

Early in 1967 Dudley's passenger station was being demolished, and it was reported that the Freightliner Depot, costing £250,000 would be completed by the autumn.

As the depot took shape and the track layout was rationalised, the existing signal boxes were closed and a new Dudley Signal Box was opened on 16th July 1967. By that time the new sidings forming the container transshipment area were ready to be brought under the control of the new signal box, but services did not begin until 6th November of that year. The first train was sent on its way to Glasgow, and the depot was officially declared open by Mr.King-Farlow, President of the Birmingham Chamber of Commerce. (Why not Dudley Chamber of Commerce?)

The depot was supposed to be able to handle ten or twelve freightliner trains per day, but at first only two services were operated - to Glasgow, and to Stockton. The following year services to Harwich and Hull were introduced. In 1970 another Freightliner depot opened in Birmingham. Although traffic at Dudley was supposed to be healthy it is impossible not wonder if the depot was a failure. The interesting thing is that the closure of the old Dudley station and the opening of the Freightliner Depot, plus the need to re-route all freight through Bescot yard, re-cast the "axis" of Dudley's rail network.

Up until the mid sixties it was possible to think of Dudley as being on a north-to-south railway - the original OWWR line of 1852 vintage. The lines radiating from this north to south route, the South Staffordshire line, the Birmingham via Swan Village line, and the Old Hill line, were the appendages. After the opening of the Freightliner depot the South Staffordshire line re-asserted its importance, and it was via this line that the Freightliner trains reached the electrified north-south railway at Bescot. The section of the old OWWR north of Dudley was singled and quickly withered away - it was closed on 1st January 1968! The line south of Dudley now became an extension of the route from Bescot over which local "trip" workings and through goods traffic reached such places as Round Oak, and the yard at Kingswinford Junction. (For a time a Freightliner service did use the southern part of the OWWR line, in providing a Dudley - Swansea service.) It was in this form that enthusiasts have known the Dudley line from 1967 to 1993.

British Rail may have wished to close the Freightliner Depot in the mid 1970s, but, by coincidence, the Minister of Transport was Dudley's MP, and he was opposed to the closure. By the early 1980s it seemed as if Dudley's Freightliner traffic could be handled at the Birmingham depot at Lawley Street, but it was uncertain if customers would welcome the extra mileage by road forced upon their containers. As the Black Country began to face serious problems of recession it seemed vital to retain freight carrying infrastructure that might preserve jobs or attract new industry, and by 1983 it was agreed to keep the depot open, but also continually review the situation. By the mid 1980s only three services using the depot remained in operation, and one of the overhead cranes was out of use.

On 29th September 1986 the last train left Dudley Freightliner Depot - the 6.45.pm departure for Carlisle, via Bescot. But this was not quite the end of the story of Dudley's railway. The "South Staffordshire" tracks from Bescot to Dudley, and thence on to Round Oak, Kingswinford Junction and Stourbridge Junction continued to be used by local freight trains and by through workings travelling further afield. Dudley's "new" signal box, of 1967 vintage, remained open on a part-time basis, so Dudley was still a point on the railway map, even if shorn of every facility except the signal box.

On 5th June 1988 Dudley signal box was closed and the section of line from Eagle Crossing, near Great Bridge, to Round Oak South became one "block section". A few trains a day still trundled through Dudley - through the featureless zone that had once been station, goods yards, and freightliner depot. Dudley still had a railway - although not served by that railway!

Below: The sad state of Dudley Station in January 1967 as demolition makes way for the new Freightliner Depot. On the left is Bill Hart who had been signalman at the South Box for the previous ten years. On the right is Inspector G . Keeling.
(Photo from the collection of Mrs. Sambrook)

The final humiliation - closure of the remaining line - came on 22nd March 1993, with the last trains running on Friday 19th March. By this time even thinking of the British Rail network in terms of "regions" was "old hat". The new "business-led" railway was organised into sectors, and the line through Dudley was within the province of Trainload Freight. This sector had to meet financial targets set by central Government , and saw no point in maintaining a double track railway to carry a few trains a day to destinations south of Dudley that could be reached by alternative, although more circuitous, routes.

As usual there were a few limp protests, but few protesters were aware of how much Britain's railways had changed in the previous decade. As far as Dudley was concerned it had really lost its last tangible association with the railway in 1986 when the Freightliner depot had quietly closed. The irony is that the Black Country had changed so much in the previous decades that it was the hope of retaining the line for future passenger use that was also a feature of the closure protests.

A traffic congested, recession-battered, Black Country was looking for means of re-generation. Railway tracks and potential routes of new forms of public transport hold out some hope to planners trying to build future prosperity for the region. In some glossy dream of the Black Country's future - built on retailing, service "industries", tourism and leisure, there is a hope that we might all glide around in environmentally friendly forms of public transport. As these words are being written the rusting tracks through Dudley cease to be part of a single nationalised industry and become a closed part of the new potentially private railway. But, for the time being the tracks remain in place, a question mark hangs over their fate even as plans materialise that will alter the whole landscape of the area that once surrounded the station. For some, their existence helps maintain the vision that one day rail-based transport will once again pass Castle Hill.

For others, the story ended on 19th March 1993 when class 47 locomotive no. 47238, "Bescot Yard", passed through Dudley on its way back to Bescot, bearing the special headboard:

"The Dudley Dasher Memorial Special".

Railway enthusiast did not very systematically record the goods facilities provided at Dudley, but these two locomotive portraits contain information about such facilities within the background of the picture.

Above: Ex GWR "Hall" class 4-6-0, no.6918, "Sandon Hall", arrives at the north end of platform 2 with empty stock from Wolverhampton which will go forward from Dudley at 2.30.pm. On the right we catch a glimpse of the ex LMS goods shed and bonded warehouse. (Lawrence Brownhill)

Below: Ex LMS/LNWR "Duck Eight" 0-8-0, 48964, proudly displaying its 3A, Bescot, shed plate on the smoke box, shunts at Dudley on the lines giving access to the LMS yard. However, to the left of the locomotive we catch a glimpse of the GWR goods shed, revealing that the roof consisted of two pitches, the first covering three railway tracks, the second covering a large storage area. Despite the rather Victorian appearance of the locomotive, the picture dates from the late 1950s and platform 2 hosts a BR Western Region enamelled station name board in brown and cream. (Eric Rogers)

Track Layouts: Dudley Station

Two layouts are reproduced here, but a more comprehensive picture of the development of Dudley's layout can be gained by study of the 1:2500 Ordnance survey maps of 1887, 1919 and 1938. The Godfrey Edition of Map 67.12, dated 1901, is particularly clear. R.A.Cooke's "Track Layout Diagrams of the GWR etc," Section 31 is invaluable. To simplify matters the Tipton Road and Birmingham Road and associated overbridges have been excluded, as well as the footbridge and buidings on the station platform.

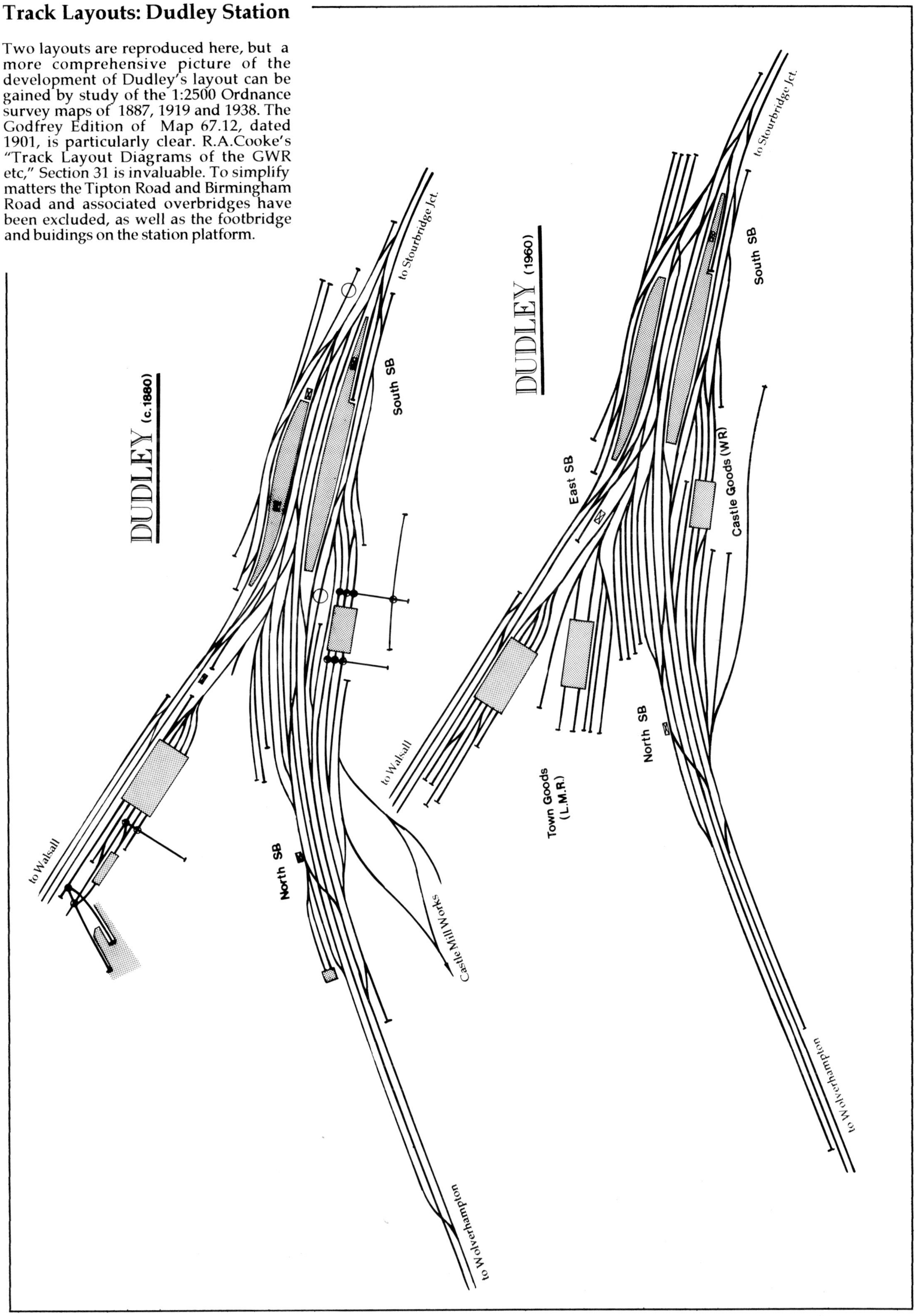

Above: Ex GWR 64xx class 0-6-0PT, 6403, stands at platform 1 on 17th May 1963 as parcels trolleys obstruct the gas lit platform and the evening sun casts its shadows across the scene. (P.J.Shoesmith)

Left: Herbert Bird collected his Cannock Chase house coals from the LNWR's wharf at Dudley Station although his office and home was, at the time, in Wellington Road. His office was the home of two large model coal wagons kept in a glass case, but we have no photographic record of his own "private owner" wagons on the railway.

Below: The name "Dudley Town" appears on this BR (Midland Region) passenger ticket - presumably to distinguish the town's station from the station at Dudley Port, from which this4d journey commenced - unless there was a time when the LMR side of the station was known officially as "Dudley Town"?

General Views of Dudley Station

The obvious place from which to take photographs of Dudley Station was from the road bridge overlooking the south end of the station, or from the top of Station Drive. Above: This picture was taken just after the War, and before Nationalisation, showing platform 1 at its tidiest but the station buildings somewhat grubby compared with later pictures. (Roy Smith)

Right: This general view clearly illustrates the layout of Dudley station - two parallel island platforms, one forming the GWR station, the other the LMS. By the time this picture was taken nationalisation had brought the entire station under the control of British Railways, but "separation" continued in the form of the Western Region and the London Midland Region, until "united" within the LM Region in January 1963. The GWR and LMS/LNWR traditions are represented in this picture by the ex GWR diesel railcar standing in the bay platform on the left, and the ex LNWR G2 0-8-0 emerging with a freight train from the right hand side of the station. (John Dew)

Right: Ex GWR Prairie class 51xx, 4114, shedded at Kidderminster, leaves Platform 5 on the LMR side of the station with the 17.35.pm. Birmingham Snow Hill - Brettell Lane train, made up of four coaches, on 13th September 1961. (Normally it was the 18.05.pm. from Snow Hill which was the booked turn of the Kidderminster based engine.) Note on the extreme left of the Booking Hall that the canopy over Station Drive is still extant. In later views the canopy appears to be removed. (George Bennett)

The South end of Dudley Station

Left: Looking south from the LMS platform on 17th May 1963, beneath the footbridge, gives a good view of Dudley South Signal Box, the Birmingham Road overbridge, and the cutting forming the approach to the tunnel. (P.J.Shoesmith)

Left: Dudley South Signal Box stood at the southern end of the GWR platform, and had been strengthened by a brick "skirt" giving it a somewhat massive appearance. Its accessibility from the platform (Dudley's other two boxes were quite remote from the platforms) made it a mecca for local railway enthusiasts, and its signalmen became well known to them. (George Bennett)

Left: Signalman Bill Hart stands at the window of Dudley South Box as ex LMS class 2 2-6-0, 46490, of Bescot Shed, shunts some parcels vans which will form the evening parcels trip to Dudley Port High Level in 1963. (George Bennett)

Dudley - the GWR Side.

Right: Ex GWR "Grange" class 4-6-0, 6845, "Paviland Grange", of Tyseley Shed, prepares to depart from Platform 2 with a zoo excursion returning to Great Malvern, on 3rd. August 1964, by which time all regular passenger services serving Dudley station had been withdrawn. For some reason there were less Western Region specials to the zoo than LM region ones, and the locomotives on the WR excursions would have had to return to Stourbridge Shed for turning and preparation for the homeward journey. (George Bennett)

Right: Ex GWR 64xx class 0-6-0PT, 6434, of Stourbridge Shed propels auto trailer W254W back to Stourbridge Junction as "empty stock", having just provided the 7.00.pm service from Old Hill to Dudley - the final passenger carrying journey over the line on the penultimate day of operation - Friday 12th June 1964. (George Bennett)

Right: Normally auto-coach W254W had the "driving end" facing Old Hill, but in this photograph the coach is facing the other way! The locomotive is class 64xx 0-6-0PT no.6403. 17th May 1963. (P.J.Shoesmith)

Dudley - LMS Side

Left: The ExLMS, ex LNWR, platform at Dudley as seen from the ex GWR platform looking northwards in October 1952. Note that the canopy continues north of the station master's office, and appears cut back in later photographs. On the side wall of the staircase down to the LMS platform the LMS erected a large sign facing the GWR platform saying: "This side for New Street Station - Birmingham", to remind GWR passengers that Snow Hill was not the only station in Brum. (Tim Shuttleworth)

Left: Ex LMS 2-4-2T, 46712, still in LMS livery, waits to leave the LMS platform at Dudley with the 5.05. pm. train to Walsall, propelling "The Dudley Dasher" push-pull train and towing a parcels van. (W.A.Camwell)

Below: The last scheduled passenger train from Dudley to Birmingham Snow Hill, the 8.10.pm. waits to leave the LMS platform on Sunday evening 14th June 1964. (The train is seen again at the foot of page 20 at the start of its journey.) Dudley Hippodrome and its huge fly tower dominate the background, plus the back of the Plaza cinema. One proposed line of the Midland Metro would enter Dudley via the "South Staffs" line and then climb into the town of Dudley itself by skirting past the back of the Plaza cinema. (Michael Mensing)

The North End

Above: Ex GWR 57xx class 0-6-0PT, 4665, arrives at Dudley with the 12.03.pm. (Saturdays only) train from Wolverhampton LL to Dudley and Old Hill on 21st July 1962. At Old Hill this train formed the 12.45. return trip to Dudley. Dudley East signal Box and the lines disappearing beneath the Tipton Road bridge are visible on the right. (Ron Hartshorne)

Right: Arriving at the north end of the LMS platform at Dudley, on 22nd June 1963, is an SLS special behind Ex LMS G2 0-8-0, 49361. On the left is the LM Region goods station, "Dudley Town", which, at this time, included bonded warehouse facilities for Messrs Rutland & Lett. (John Dew)

Right: Dudley East Signal Box. On the extreme right of this picture it is possible to see the "tunnel" beneath the Dudley - Tipton Road that gave access to the goods facilities on the far side of the road
(George Bennett)

Zoo Specials

Left: Dudley East Signal Box fills the centre of this picture, taken in April 1961, as Easter Zoo specials fill the station. An ex LMS 2-6-0, 42823, is just leaving the station with a special returning to Derby.
(W.A.Camwell)

Left: Two Easters earlier, ex LMS "Crab" 2-6-0, 42897, is seen arriving in Dudley with a Zoo Excursion of coaches in the "blood and custard". The track, on the right, to the LMS loading dock later provided access to the new signal box built in 1967. The photographically elusive Dudley North signal box can just be seen on the centre of the skyline of this picture. (W.A.Camwell)

Left: Zoo excursions also came through to Dudley from the Eastern Region of British Railways. Ex LNER class B1 4-6-0, 61223, of Lincoln Shed, arrives with such a train on 22nd April 1962. After depositing its empty stock in the middle road, or in the Western Region half of the station, the engine would return tender-first to Bescot for turning and preparation for the return journey. On that particular day excursions came to Dudley from Lincoln, Nottingham, Doncaster and Derby.
(Eric Rogers/Lawrence Brownhill)

SLS Enthusiasts' Specials

Right: BR standard class 9F 2-10-0, 92113, and Rebuilt Merchant Navy class 4-6-2, 35026, "Lamport & Holt Line" draw "The Aberdonian" railtour through Dudley on 26th June 1966, emerging from the LMS half of the station and passing their Palethorpes Sausages vans at the southern end of the station. The special train then traversed the Bumble Hole line.
(Martin Shenton)

Right: Ex GWR Prairie 2-6-2T, 4555, owned by Patrick Whitehouse and Patrick Garland, brought an SLS special into Dudley, having just traversed the Bumble Hole line on 13 th June 1964 - the day the line closed to passengers. The train continued to Wolverhampton southwards over the Wombourn branch. (Ron Moss)

Right: An SLS double headed special was photographed leaving Dudley and heading for the tunnel on 11th September 1966. The Stephenson Locomotive Society promoted the trip as a "Farewell to GWR 0-6-PTs", and of the two locomotives, 9630 and 9610, the latter made its own "farewell" gesture later in the day by failing at Lapworth!
(John Harris)

Around the Yards

Above: Dudley Castle Goods Station. After nationalisation it became essential to differentiate between the various goods facilities provided at Dudley. The LMS yard became Dudley Town and the GWR yard became Dudley Castle - as seen here on the board carried by the goods offices. Although it seems doubtful that the passenger facilities were differentiated in the same way, it is interesting to note the ticket reproduced below does use the term "Dudley Town". In this case it may be used to distinguis the town's station from "Dudley Port".
(C.B.Roberts)

Left: Loading docks were an essential feature of any self-respecting station, some being added as recently as the First World War for the dispatch of the cavalry. In the absence of any other use the short dock in Dudley Castle Yard is seen here providing accommodation for the push-pull unit W225W, about 1961. Behind the coach, and in front of the trees of Castle Hill, stands the long wooden goods shed that became a banana warehouse in the early 1960s. (George Bennett)

Left: The last scheduled passenger train leaves Dudley for Birmingham on 14th June 1964 at 8.10.pm. The train consists of a single car diesel unit W 55018 plus two thirds of a WR suburban DMU, plus a complete three car WR suburban DMU. The train has just passed under the Tipton Road bridge and is descending the bank to Sedgeley Junction, Dudley Port Low Level, Great Bridge South, Swan Village, and off to Birmingham Snow Hill. In the background are the goods sidings of the LMS (Ex LNWR) goods yard. The LNWR goods shed stood between the running lines and the buttressed wall on the right. Two tracks disappeared beneath the brick store on the right, the top surface of which seems to have formed a cartage area. A stable block can be seen at Tipton Road level. Beyond is the outline of the shed on the far side of the Tipton Road, normally seen in distant front elevation in photographs looking north from Dudley station. Somewhere up in the trees of Castle Hill is the Zoo Miniature Railway!
(Michael Mensing)

Vans and Parcels Traffic

Right: A colourful feature of railway life at Dudley was the coming and going of Palethorpes Sausage vans. The company had their own siding not far from Sedgeley Junction Signal Box on the South Staffs line - but on the wrong side of the junction for straightforward access to Dudley Port and the main line. Even LMS-bound vans had to come up to Dudley therefore in order to be taken back to Dudley Port High Level. The company had used rail transport and "private owner vans" since LNWR days and adopted very distinctive bright red four and six wheel vans in LMS days. In this picture it is possible to see two types of bogie vehicle, as well as the six wheeler. The bogie vans are parked in the sidings that had once been in the LNWR locomotive shed, and were latterly used as carriage sidings. Note the huge wall of hoardings lining the Tipton Road and adding emphasis to the impression that Dudley Station was in a deep chasm, in this view from platform 2, in 1962. (George Bennett)

Right: Looking across the northern end of the LMS platform from platform 2 reveals the presence of another interesting van at Dudley, sometime in 1962. The Anglo-Scottish Car Carrier van and its Eastern Region neighbour have slipped into Dudley among the many movements of vans between Dudley and Dudley Port High Level. The picture also reveals the end wall of the wooden buildings on the LMS platform, including the door to the Station Master's Office. A canopy extended forward from this building, and the marks on the platform's surface indicate the former position of four stanchions. George Bennett)

Below: Ex LMS class 2 2-6-0, no. 46490, stands at the LMS platform with a short parcels train in the early evening of 17th May 1963. In the distance it is possible to see Kates Hill and St.John's Church. (Parliamentary forces are said to have laid siege to Dudley Castle from a position on Kates Hill.) (P.J.Shoesmith)

Out with the "old". In with the "new".

Left: In January 1967 a class 47 diesel locomotive passes through platform 2 at Dudley Station (in the days when diesels were two-tone green and carried reporting numbers), while the station was being demolished and the track layout and signalling re-organised. (John Harris)

Left: A Wolverhampton-built Guy articulated lorry and its container load poses at the Dudley Freightliner Depot to demonstrate the "system" to new customers. The Dudley Freightliner Terminal was the first such depot to open in the West Midlands - and opened on 6th November 1967. An integrated "door to door" road and rail container service with twenty four hour delivery time was expected to win much freight traffic to the railways.The containers travelled on permanently coupled flat wagons, and were lifted into place with giant overhead cranes, the road vehicles circulated through the depot on a one-way system. Freightliners Ltd was formed in January 1969 to assume responsibility for such operations, and on the 3rd November of that year a second depot was opened at Landor Street, Birmingham. To some extent the growth in traffic was never sufficient to fully justify the existence of both depots, plus the growth of specialist steel terminals etc.

Below: A class 40 locomotive, 40 012, stands in the Freightliner Depot in the early 1980s when the future of the Depot seemed uncertain. The new signal box, on the right of the picture, had opened in July 1967 in anticipation of the completion of the depot.
(Brian Robbins)

Castles and Closures

Right: The site of Dudley Station on 8th May 1984: Class 58, 58 002, pulls class 86, 86 245 from the up line on to the down line and thence into the Freightliner Depot, as the linesman descends the steps from the signal box. Later 86 245 was named "Dudley Castle" by the Earl of Dudley, and as an electric locomotive marooned far from any overhead wire it had to be towed back to Bescot. The Earl of Dudley in his speech was able to refer to the earlier carrier of this name: GWR "Castle" class locomotive no.4091. (Ned Williams)

Centre: The last Freightliner train from Dudley Freightliner Depot ran on 29th September 1986, with very little public attention or protest. The railway staff attached a wreath to the front of locomotive 58 030 to mark the occasion, and Driver Bill Allsworth and Guard Derek Hillman posed in front of the locomotive before it departed with the 6.45.pm train to Bescot going forward to Carlisle. (Brian Robbins)

Below: Dudley Signal Box was taken out of use on 5th June 1988 and a new block section was established running from Eagle Crossing to Round Oak South. A month later vandals set fire to the box and destroyed it. This robbed Dudley of its one "feature" from a railway photographer's point of view, and when the line closed altogether on 19th March 1993 it was noticeable that very few photographers chose to record the events of the last day at Dudley itself. This picture - taken on that "last day" - shows class 37 locomotive, 37 884, "Gartcosh", passing through the stripped and bare landscape of the Dudley station site with steel for Brierley Hill Terminal (Moor Lane). (Ned Williams)

Outside Dudley Station

Dudley Station, at the foot of Castle Hill, was always regarded as being rather remote from Dudley's town centre, The distance probably seemed greater before Castle Hill itself was built upon. In this picture, taken in the 1890s, the slopes of Castle Hill are still tree-covered and devoid of buildings. A Dudley & Stourbridge Steam Tramway Co.'s tram locomotive and trailer have halted at the terminus opposite the entrance to Station Drive, serving the GWR side of the station. Pillars, gates and lamps add to the imposing appearance of the entrance to Station Drive and two boards advertise the railway's services. The tram locomotive is about to run round the trailer car to return to Stourbridge. The double track down Castle Hill singled in the foreground and curved into the depot overlooking the station. The track continuing towards the camera links the D & SST with the South Staffordshire Tramways' lines to Tipton and the Birmingham and Midland Tramways line to Birmingham. (Collection of Stan Webb)

Left: The foot of Castle Hill about 1910 as South Staffs Brush-built electric car no.23 waits to depart from outside Dudley station to Handsworth via B & MT track - a service which had been electrified since May 1903. On the left is the Station Hotel, and on the right, close to the entrance to Station Drive, is The Dudley Opera House, opened by John Maurice Clement in September 1899. The gates and boards at the top of Station Drive do not seem to have changed over the decade that has elapsed since the above picture was taken. (Collection of Stan Webb)

Left:This picture was taken on 13th September 1938 - The Station Hotel still looks much the same but the opposite side of Castle Hill has been transformed by the opening of the Zoo, the building of the Plaza cinema, the burning down of the Opera House and the building of its replacement - the "New Opera House", which was to become "The Hippodrome" when it opened a few months later. Hoardings have been erected on the parapet of the railway bridge, including a Palethorpes Sausage advert. Since 1924 the trams from Birmingham had been provided by Birmingham Corporation Tramways, and in the following years the electric routes through Dudley closed. In 1930 the remaining services down the Tipton Road to Wednesbury closed, leaving only the BCT's trams terminating at the foot of Castle Hill. On the left car no.154 on the 87 route to Birmingham via Oldbury, and behind it is a bogie car on the 74 route via West Bromwich. These routes closed in 1939.

Road transport was always a serious competitor with rail when it came to journeys between Dudley and Birmingham, and the buses which replaced the trams had the advantage of terminating closer to the centre of town. (W.A.Camwell)

Dudley Station Remembered 1938 - 1941

An article by **Kenneth Tibbetts** that first appeared in The Blackcountryman Vol 26 no.4, Autumn 1993.

It is thirty years since Dudley ceased to have passenger trains, and it is hard to imagine now what a busy, bustling station it was when I began to work there as a junior clerk in February 1938. On a normal weekday over 140 trains departed from the station between 5.00.am and 11.30.pm. There were something like 50 trips to Dudley Port High Level, and another 16 trains to Walsall calling at the Low Level station at Dudley Port. On the GW line about 20 trains a day went to Birmingham Snow Hill via Swan Village and West Bromwich , and there were two dozen trips to Old Hill. In addition there were regular services on the line from Wolverhampton Low Level to Stourbridge Junction. One of the Wolverhampton trains was an express of sorts to Crewe using the little known Wellington to Nantwich line. Of the Stourbridge trains, some went through to Worcester, and two right through to Paddington via Oxford. Of the many cheap workmen's tickets issued before 8.00.am. each morning, no less than 240 were to Birmingham Snow Hill. Indeed, passengers for the two most popular Snow Hill trains came in such a rush that tickets were sold from both the GW and LMS windows.

Passengers entered the station by a covered footbridge that stretched across both the GW and LMS platforms, running from the approach road beneath Castle Hill to an entrance on the Tipton Road. The footbridge began as a fairly spacious booking hall, with two ticket windows immediately on the left, the LMS one first, the GWR one further along. Beyond that was a staircase leading to the GWR platform, with a ticket collector's cabin at its head. (There was another staircase opposite that had long been out of use.) This part of the structure was built in blue brick externally, as were all the main buildings on the GWR platform. The rest of the footbridge was of timber construction, and so were the buildings on the LMS platform. Beyond the staircase to the LMS platform, at the Tipton Road end of the bridge was the parcels office.

Among the buildings on the GWR platform was a licensed refreshment room, and the LMS platform had a Wyman's bookstall. At the north end of the LMS platform was the Station Master's Office. Above the mantle piece in this office was a framed list of the departures from Dudley from a date in the late 1850s, and it was headed "South Staffordshire Railway".

My railway career lasted little more than three and a half years, and apart from a short spell at Tipton, it was spent entirely at Dudley station. I was employed by the LMS company, but in 1938 clerks from both the LMS and GWR worked side by side in the one large booking office, with its two ticket windows - one for each company. Any of us could appear at either of those windows and we all had to be conversant with two different ways of doing things, and two different accounting systems. Indeed, in the very early morning, and after 6.00.pm. only one clerk was on duty. Passengers were often surprised - and not always pleased - to be asked to "go to the other window", only to see the same face there. During 1939 the GWR clerks were withdrawn, and under a closer working arrangement, the LMS manned both sides of the office. Up until then the Chief Clerk, Mr.Jesse Williams, had been a GW man, and the last two GW clerks had been Victor Rowen and Eric Short. I understand that the wheel turned full circle, and in later years the station was staffed entirely by "Western" men.

The "closer working arrangement" of 1939 applied only to the booking office. As for platform foremen, porters, signalmen, shunters etc., the two sides of the station continued to be manned by the two separate companies.

The office was staffed by a total of nine clerks, four of whom worked on a complicated system of shifts. One clerk, Arthur Limb, was engaged entirely on matters relating to dispatch, from both Dudley and Dudley Port, of Palethorpes' sausage traffic. In addition, a further two clerks, Fred Bates and Maurice Allen, working shifts, manned the Parcels Office at the Tipton Road end of the footbridge. Two motor vans and one horse-drawn van dealt with the collection and delivery of the tremendous quantity of parcels that passed through the office each day.

I was quite surprised when I began working there to find that nearly all the clerks wore hats - a selection of trilbys and bowlers - all day long in the office. It may have been because quite a draught blew through the ticket windows. One of my colleagues was completely bald, but I had been there nearly a year before I discovered it!

The Station Master, Mr. H. Hayward, was an LMS man, reared on the Midland Railway. As Dudley was deservedly considered such an important station, his position was a "special grade" appointment. His uniform was as splendid as an admiral's, and bore the gold-embroidered legend, "LMS & GW Joint". He was very much an autocrat, but was extremely kind to me when, as a junior, I spent a couple of hours each afternoon in his office, helping with his correspondence, and with numerous records and returns, thus gaining a deep insight into railway operating in general.

Looking back on those three and a half years, I have always felt fortunate that I worked at a station like Dudley, where we were called upon to tackle such a variety of things that days were rarely boring. Apart from issuing tickets and dealing with enquiries about train services, we dealt with working out and paying wages for the platform, yard and signal box staff - again for two different companies with two different systems. We also did spells of relieving or assisting in the Parcels Office.

The telephone seemed to be ringing all day - mainly with enquiries - but, in addition, there was a group of internal railway phones, one for the LMS and three for the GWR. These linked together groups of stations and signal boxes, each being summoned by its own bell-code. So, all day long, these phones were buzzing away, our ears deaf to them except when our own code (4 - 1) was rung. It was possible to to listen in to other conversations, or for several of us to have a chat together. At 12.00. all the GWR phones sounded an imperious sequence of buzzes in unison to give us a daily time check from Paddington.

Each of these GW phones included Snow Hill station on its circuit and Snow Hill had a direct line to New Street, the GWR and LMS stations in Birmingham. So, one could could ring Snow Hill and be ask to be put through to New Street, and then ask to be connected to an LMS station. Once, in a quiet spell, a colleague named Tom Cartwright, and I tried the experiment of using this link to speak to each other. We stood, a few feet apart, and held a telephone conversation with over twenty miles of railway telephone wire connecting us!

But there were comparatively few quiet spells until mid evening, as we never went for very long without there being someone at one or other of the windows, booking tickets or making travel enquiries. Numerous places could be reached by the lines of either company - Birmingham, Wolverhampton, London and the south coast, Bristol, Chester, even Swansea by the unlikely LMS route via Stafford, Shrewsbury and Craven Arms, so there was a friendly rivalry between the clerks manning the two windows.

In the course of time, one developed an amazing knowledge of railway geography, and an astonishing memory for train times and connections. However, there were gaps, sometimes culpable, in that knowledge. One Sunday evening I issued a first class single to Stourbridge Town to a top executive of Marsh & Baxter's. I had failed to remember that there were no Sunday trains from Stourbridge Junction to Stourbridge Town. The poor man had to complete his journey by taxi, and wrote an angry letter claiming a refund. I was duly reprimanded in writing of course, and my colleagues delighted in quoting to me frequently one sentence from his letter: "To issue tickets to stations that are closed is deplorable!"

The LMS trains from Walsall were shown in the timetable as connecting with the GWR trains to Stourbridge and beyond, but sometimes they failed to do so. The headmistress of a private school in Walsall frequently used to travel to Arley on the Severn Valley line. (We supposed that she was travelling to the private school at Arley Court.) To do this, her train from Walsall had to connect with the 8.49 to Kidderminster, and she made a tremendous fuss if the train had gone without her. Sometimes we would receive a warning phone call from Walsall: "First Class for Arley Castle en route!"

On Sunday mornings there was frequently much activity in dispatching baskets of homing pigeons to various destinations, the birds to be released on arrival. As the Parcels Office was closed, the baskets were brought to the Booking Office door to be charged and stamped. Most summer Sundays saw numerous cheap excursions, particularly on the GW side, but is was Bank Holiday excursions that attracted really large crowds of extra passengers, and we could be rushed off our feet all morning. There were excursions into Dudley too, long trains often bringing Bank Holiday visitors to Dudley Zoo.

Another time of unusual activity was early September when the platform was crowded day after day with families, many with battered tin trunks, off for several weeks hop-picking in and around the Teme valley. A number of special trains were run to convey them, and in most cases they presented vouchers issued by the hop-yard owners in payment for their journeys. That annual hop-picking exodus is now an almost forgotten thing of the past.

It is also easy to forget how many people would take advantage of cheap evening tickets to go into Wolverhampton or Birmingham at tea-time for a few hours around the shops which kept open until 8.00.pm, and even 9.00.pm. on Saturdays. And it is difficult to imagine a commuter "rush hour" at Dudley's station each morning and night, but here are two illustrations of how busy we were. One of the two GWR ticket collectors was nearing the end of his career and could not cope with the tea-time rush. Scores of people, returning from work, would rush up the stairs and dash past him, throwing their tickets into his cabin. He would then spend the evening sorting through them, often ending up with a pile that were invalid or on which an excess should have been paid. He would then bring these tickets into the office, and throw them onto the fire saying, "A few more for the Clearing House!"

We faced similar problems in the mornings. There was a very busy train around 7.00.am. Factory and office workers would come running down the drive at the very last moment or even later. They would give their money to one of their number, and run down to the platform to hold back the train. Their friend would come to the booking office window and bang down a pile of varied coins, and demand something like, "Four Soho, seven Snow Hill and six Small Heath." We would issue the required tickets, and then, when she had gone, we were left hoping that the cash would be correct. Often it was not - and it could well be that they found they had the wrong selection of tickets!

Tickets for GWR journeys could also be bought, and other business transacted, at the "Town Office" in Castle Street. This was run by Mr.H.E.Thomas, as a private agency, though his takings were incorporated into the station accounts at the end of each month. Frames Tours acted in a similar, but separate, way for the LMS.

Apart from our passenger station, each company had its own separate goods depots - the GWR one further down the station drive, beneath Castle Hill, the LMS one in Tipton Road. As Dudley was a junction station, wagons were transferred from one company to the other in exchange sidings, to become part of freshly-marshalled trains. The Station Master spent a large slice of his day supervising these operations, and two clerks were employed by the Railway Clearing House to record the the ownership and number of every wagon transferred. They were housed in a small office at the north end of the GW platform.

Our internal phones conveyed frequent enquiries, in telegram form, about wagons which were late in reaching their destinations, and each such enquiry required a visit to the Railway Clearing House office to search through their register. Sometimes I had to venture into the shunters' cabin, tiptoeing perilously between sidings and wagons. These quite frequent errands were not just an escape from the office for a few minutes - they also provided direct contact with the wider activity of the railway system.

The two different accounting systems used by the two companies also involved different ways of remitting the takings. Each week-day one of the senior clerks, usually Jim Edwards, went to a bank in the town to pay in the previous day's LMS receipts, but the GWR cash was sent direct to the District Cashier at Worcester. For this purpose, a travelling safe was conveyed in the guard's van of the 8.49. train every morning, and at each station a padlocked leather pouch containing the previous day's cash was inserted. The pouch was actually prepared by the chief clerk on the previous afternoon and placed in the office safe. Then, for greater security, it was transferred each night to a safe provided in the South Signal Box at the end of the GW platform. So, when I was working the late shift, I would choose a quiet half hour in the late evening to walk along to the box with it, and stay watching the signalman at work or chat over a cup of tea. (One of the men in that box was a prominent Dudley Councillor - Alderman W.C. Williams, who had been Mayor in 1933-34.) It was these regular visits to the signal box that gave me a life-long interest in railway signalling.

One of the 'perks' of working on the railway was the entitlement to cheap travel and six free tickets a year. I made full use of these privileges, but I was amazed to find that one of our senior clerks never applied for more than one free ticket a year - a return from Dudley to Rugeley for his annual leave! This journey would have cost a member of the public less than three shillings.

In October 1941 my railway career came to an end when National Service claimed me. After the War, my life took a different turn, but railways had got 'into my blood', and the 'infection' has been never left me. I never imagined that a day would come when not a stone remained of those blue-brick buildings where I spent three and a half years.

* * * * * * *

Left: A Park Royal 2-car DMU leaves Dudley as the 5.18 pm train to Walsall on 2nd May 1964 - the last summer the serivce operated. This view from the Tipton Road bridge looking into the northern end of Dudley Station shows the booking hall and buildings on the ex GWR platform, but it also shows the parcels lorry depot by the zoo car park, and to the right, behind the Eastern Region coaches and the yard crane there is just a glimpse of the "banana" shed - rarely seen in photographs as it lay so far back from the rest of the railway. (Michael Mensing)

A Signalman Remembers

Edgar Rumble

Recorded 18th. March 1994

I started on the railway in August 1942 at Stourbridge Junction as a telephonist, and did various jobs there; porter, booking office dog's body, booking lad in Stourbridge North Signal Box, lampman, passenger shunter etc. I left there in 1947 and went into Baggeridge Junction Box, then to Round Oak North in 1948 and on to Blowers Green Sidings in 1950. I became a rest-day relief signalman in 1960, and was a relief signalman until I retired in 1993.

During my career as a relief signalman I went to most of the boxes in the area,including the boxes at Dudley. My first memory of going to Dudley was going to Dudley East Signal Box, which was a "foreign" box to someone brought up on the Western! My first memory of this was going up the steps and finding that the door opened outwards - which of course was not "right", and then I saw the frame that one couldn't walk on, because the runners for the levers stood proud of the frame. The only bloke who could walk on the frame was Cliff Talbot because he'd got two left feet. He was also a Western man, in fact the only ex LMS man around at the time was Ernie Bill who had been the LMS man in the East Box when it was taken over. He then went to the North Box, and then to the South Box - so he never left Dudley, but he worked in all three boxes. The last signalman to work at the East box was a chap called Micky Willis.

Although I did not spend a great deal of time on relief in the South Box, I knew it from time spent hand signalling, and by "visiting" the box. It was a class 1 box, and was by far the busiest box at Dudley. It handled all the trains coming into Dudley from the Blowers Green end, plus the trains from Wolverhampton and the trains from Birmingham via Great Bridge. There were two passenger trains in the morning which came from the Stourbridge direction making for Birmingham. The first started from Stourbridge, but the other worked as empty stock from Stourbridge and picked up its first passengers at Brettell Lane -it was the 6.37.am ex Brettell Lane - Birmingham train!

These two trains came into the Western side of the station and then reversed before making their way on to Birmingham via the Midland side of the station - and there were two workings in the other direction in the evening, but no reversal was necessary during the evening. They were usually worked by class 51 or 41 2-6-2 tanks. Two freights from the Stourbridge direction in the early hours that were transferring to the Midland also had to run into the station and then reverse before gaining access to the Midland metals, on the down main or down goods lines. One was a Gloucester - Bescot service, the other was Bristol - Bescot. I can remember that if the second one didn't get up to Dudley by 5.30.am it would have to wait until after 9.30., as we were too busy dealing with passenger trains to deal with it.

Although the South box was busy, it was always operated by one signalman, to my knowledge, without even a booking lad. In my day all trace of the LNWR box at that end of the station had long since disappeared, but legend had it that in the old days the signalmen had been able to shout back and forth to each other. Both the South and North boxes were standard Western boxes, but the South box was slightly unusual as it had a thick "blast" wall built round it just before the War, and, of course, it stood on the platform, only four steps up from the platform.

When we took over the East box it was a class 3 box, and a lot of men worked there briefly using it as a stepping stone to get back into a class 2 box on the Western - there were always vacancies at that box! When I first went to the East box there was no permanent signalman there at all: just two or three relief men doing mostly twelve hour turns. Of course Dudley East was a grade 3 box on the Midland scheme, and legend had it that all the boxes on the Midland were a grade lower than they would have been on the Western, and that did seem likely, because, for a class 3, it did seem a pretty busy box, particularly in the daytime. As well as dealing with the passenger services from Walsall, Dudley Port, and the Birmingham service, it dealt with the transfer freights. There was a third running line from Sedgley Junction up to Dudley East, and it wasn't unusual to have two or three trains in there, waiting to get out.

Dudley North, a class 2 box, was smaller than the South box, but it was quite busy as it controlled a lot of point movement for the shunting. You certainly couldn't expect to sit down much if you were on the night shift in Dudley North. you were on your feet all night , and the shunters used to shout, "Cripple", "Middle", "Back", or whatever, and you had to pull the lever accordingly. In most yards the points would have been changed by hand using the lever adjacent to the point, but at Dudley North the points were controlled from the box. It was mainly traffic that was being exchanged from one region to the other, brought in and out by the trip workings from Oxley and Stourbridge. The Midland's trip

Right: A newspaper photograph of Alderman W.C. Williams on duty in the Dudley South Box in 1933. William "Charlie" Williams was one of several local railwaymen who went into local politics, and was Mayor of Dudley, 1933-1934. He was also a prominent member of Dudley Co-operative Society, and was the Society's President at the end of the 1930s, and while in office opened the Society's new "emporium" opposite Top Church.
(Collection of Eddy Austin)

workings were identified by number rather than by yard of origin so we didn't always know where they came from, although most came from Bescot.

There was some goods traffic specifically to Dudley, including the banana traffic which came to the long wooden shed beneath Castle Hill. They arrived looking rather green and were put through an oven to ripen them so that they were looking just right as they were sent out to the shops. Sometimes there were two or three consignments per day - in the steam-heated vans which had to be shunted into the shed. Coal was also delivered to Dudley, and there was a hopper at the back of the North box, and traffic was delivered to the Bonded Store in the Midland goods shed. Sometimes flour was delivered to that shed, and if they made a rough shunt a cloud of white dust would go up - that's how you knew flour was arriving. Sets would also arrive for the shows at Dudley Hippodrome, and every now and again elephants would arrive if the show was a circus. The station itself also dealt with a lot of parcels traffic.

Before my time there had been horse shunting at Dudley in the area around the shed that became the banana shed, and the stables were over by the Tipton Road, against the wall. I also arrived too late to know what had gone on in the goods buildings on the far side of the Tipton Road. All I can remember being kept there were some coach chassis. They were later taken down to Princes End to be converted into flat trucks.

When the new box opened in Dudley in 1967 the three signalmen who transferred to it were Bill Hart, Ernie Bill, and Trevor Jones, and, of course it was another "foreign" box as far as I was concerned. I also worked in the new box built for the Freightliner Depot. I suppose I have the distinction of being the last BR signalman to retire from Dudley box - even though I retired after the box had gone! Even with no box and not many trains it was still my "home station". As a relief signalman I continued to be paid for travel from Dudley to wherever I was working.

The Station Master was in charge of the station, but the signalman was in charge of his box and all that was associated with it. In over-all charge was the District Inspector. Even so Station Master Millington used to visit the boxes every day.

Apart from that, a signalman's main contact was with the shunters and the men in the surrounding boxes via the telephone - especially when we had the telephone system where the lines could be kept open to a number of boxes. With that system you knew what was happening well in advance. When they brought the new type phones in you could only talk to one chap at a time, and if he was on the phone when you wanted him, you couldn't get him.

Because Dudley was higher than the surrounding area, many freight trains had to be banked to Dudley. In my time a banker was stationed at Great Bridge, both day and night, to assist trains climbing to Dudley from that direction, but in later years the banker was stationed at somewhere like Perry Bar, and had to cover a wide area. It was nothing to have a freight standing at Great Bridge for an hour waiting for the banker! Coming from the other direction, when Blowers Green closed the bankers had to join their trains at Stourbridge.

It is difficult now to imagine Dudley on a bank holiday with anything up to ten special trains arriving for the Zoo, plus the diesel multiple units from Walsall and Birmingham. Mind you, even on a normal day the old GW railcar would come in from Birmingham and when the passengers poured out onto the platform you would wonder where they had all come from. There must have been ten sitting with the driver!

Once or twice things did go wrong at Dudley. For example, on one occasion we had the tunnel blocked. The train came up to Dudley with a banker, and the banker must have been pushing a bit too hard and lifted a wagon off the road, the banker dropped back and the train went on into the tunnel, and the wagons ended up all over the place, scraping the sides of the tunnel. On 11th august 1966 I was spare at Kidderminster Junction and was called up to Dudley that afternoon as soon as it happened, and worked until about eleven o'clock that night. It took two or three days for the tunnel to be cleared.

Below: An ex GWR "Mogul" 43xx pauses in front of the site of the LNWR engine shed, while collecting Palethorpes Sausage vans for a southward journey, about 1960. (Eric Rogers)

Bottom of page: A brand new "Western" diesel locomotive, D1004, "Western Crusader" brings the 8.00.am Stourbridge Jct. - Wolverhampton LL local train out of Dudley and across the Birmingham New Road in May 1962 on a crew-training run.

Note the advert for Marsh's sausages. The town of Dudley was flanked by sausage - makers: Palethorpes at Tipton, and Marsh's at Brierley Hill. (George Bennett)

Dudley in Colour

Right: Preserved ex GWR "Prairie" 2-6-2T, 4555, arrives in Dudley with the SLS Special of 13th June 1964, having just traversed the Bumble Hole line behind the last regular passenger service over the line. In this view, looking south, it is possible to see the South Box, the Birmingham Road overbridge and the retaining walls which form a backdrop to so many pictures taken at Dudley. (Geoff Bannister)

Right: A view from track level looking north at the southern end of the station as ex LMS Stanier class 8F 2-8-0 48705 passes Dudley South Signal Box with an Oxley-Stourbridge freight special, possibly with wagons bound for for Round Oak Steel Works. This picture was taken about 1965, after all passenger services had ceased. In the background note that the canopy of the Station Drive entrance to the booking hall has already gone. (John Harris)

Right: Dudley Station continued to handle parcels traffic after the various local passenger services had ceased. In another picture taken in 1965, we find BR "Standard" class 5 4-6-0, 73097, leaving its parcels train in the up platform as it goes forward to pick up a Palethorpes van from the bay, on the afternoon Wolverhampton - Stourbridge Jct. service. (John Harris)

Left: This picture is a sequel to the picture printed at the foot of the previous page. 73097, having added a van to its train, leaves Dudley, passing under the Birmingham Road Bridge and passes the water tank, making its way towards Dudley Tunnel. (John Harris)

Left: Ex LMS class 8F 2-8-0, 48680, climbs towards the Tipton Road overbridge and Dudley Station on 4th June 1963 with a Hednesford - Stourport train of "slack" for power station consumption. (The 8F, of Bescot Shed, will work the train through to Hartlebury.) The train is coming off the goods loop line, which it has occupied from Sedgeley Junction, and is being banked by "Super D" 0-8-0, 49361. Note the remains of the LNWR goods facilities in the background, the slender overbridge that once carried a colliery tramway, and the signal gantry - the two main arms protecting the platform roads, and the shorter posts carrying arms protecting the through "goods only" roads. (John Harris)

Left: Views of Dudley North Box are rare, but this picture, taken in the summer of 1966, looks across the tracks of the Dudley - Wolverhampton line and captures the height and "isolation" of the box. Class 57xx 0-6-0PT, 9774, is seen working a Stourbridge Junction - Princes End pick-up freight. This was a Tyesley-based engine far from home, as Stourbridge shed had closed by this time. (John Harris)

Right: Class 37 diesel locomotive 37 180, "County of Dyfed", approaches the site of Dudley Station with the Stoke - St.Blazey china clay empties on 31st July 1986. This view compares with the picture in the centre of the opposite page. Note that all remains of the goods "loop" have disappeared beneath vegetation and a general re-profiling of the cutting. The signal gantry has disappeared, but the brick columns supporting the one-time colliery tramway still stand. On the left, the ground level arched brickwork that supported road access to the adjacent LNWR goods warehouse still exists, but the sidings that once ran into this shed have long been lifted. The scrap yard on this site appears to be alive and well, although rather empty when this picture was taken, but now the trains have gone... (Brian Robbins)

Right: Saturday 23rd April 1988 was Mid Line Network Day, and to celebrate the occasion passengers were given the opportunity of travelling over lines normally closed to passenger traffic, The train, consisting of a three car DMU in "chocolate and cream" livery and a two car DMU in BR green is seen passing through the site of Dudley Station on its way from Stafford to Stourbridge Junction. The Freightliner Depot stands empty and abandoned but the signal box can still be seen on the right. (Ned Williams)

Right: A diesel line-up at Dudley Freightliner Depot on 19th August 1986. On the left class 31, 31 412 is about to depart with "local" trip to Landore Street, and on the right class 47, 47 228, is about to depart with the train for Glasgow. The trains will pull forward from the yard, reverse to the main running lines, and then travel forward to their destinations. (Brian Robbins)

Left: The Diesel Renaissance at Round Oak: ex Round Oak Steel Works 0-4-0 DE shunter no.2 stands at Round Oak, outside the "new" rail terminal on 20th August 1986, awaiting delivery of the Powell Dyffryn steel carrying wagons - an event which was about to be video-filmed presumably to promote the use of the rail terminal. No.s 2, 5 and 7 were "in steam" for the occasion - about two weeks prior to the official opening. (Ned Williams)

Left: At the back of Round Oak Steel Works the 0-4-0 diesel electric shunters still emptied the molten slag in this spectacular fashion in the 1980s - a moment caught on a summer evening in 1981. The works closed at the end of the following year, and lay abandoned and unwanted until the Richardsons purchased the site and began the development of the Merry Hill Complex. A glide on the monorail maybe exciting but it's not as visually dramatic as emptying molten slag on the bonk. (Gordon Nutt)

Left: In the Autumn of 1980, 0-4-0 DE. no.3., made a farewell trip along the truncated "branch" to the Old Park Engineering Works, and was photographed at the buffers a few yards short of the access to the works. This line had once extended beneath the Kingswinford Road and crossed the "Old Park" itself to make its way up to the landsale wharf at Wellington Road. (Gordon Nutt)

Northern Approaches to Dudley - the GWR lines.

Right: The West Midland Line of the GWR from Wolverhampton Low Level to Stourbridge Junction entered the enlarged County Borough of Dudley at Coseley, and the County Borough boundary followed the railway for some way. Ex GWR "Manor" class 4-6-0, 7816, "Frilsham Manor" pauses at Princes End & Coseley station on 2nd December 1961, with the lunchtime train from Wolverhampton to Stourbridge Junction. The West Midland Line also had a station at Tipton Five Ways, and a canal-rail interchange basin and yard, access to which was controlled by Tipton Junction Signal Box. (John Dew)

Right: At Bloomfield there was a wagon-repair yard belonging to the South Staffordshire Wagon Co. It was established in the mid 1950s and rail access was from the West Midland Line at Princes End & Coseley. When the West Midland Line closed completely at the end of 1967, the section from Dudley to Princes End was retained for a few months to provide access to this yard. A new connection was then put in from the yard on to the Stour Valley line close to the point at which it had been crossed by the GWR line. This picture, taken on 13th January 1981, shows a Ruston & Hornsby diesel hydraulic 0-4-0 shunter (512843 of 1966) at the Princes End "end" of the yard. (Robert Selvey)

Right: This picture was taken, about 1966, from Bloomfield Junction Signal Box, a lofty LNWR box on the Stour Valley Line, looking towards the overbridge carrying the GWR West Midland Line on its way to Dudley. Ex LMS "Black 5", 4-6-0, 45122, is passing the trailing connection put into the South Staffordshire Wagon Co.'s yard. (Lawrence Brownhill)

Northern Approaches to Dudley - the LMS lines

Left: An EMU on a Stafford - Birmingham local service approaches Dudley Port on the high level "Stour Valley" line as class 31 31 422 (and 31 155 at the rear) appears on a cable-laying train on the closed Bescot - Dudley line on 1st July 1993 - three months after the line's official closure! The cable laying train is passing the site of Dudley Port Low Level. Dudley Port has never been in Dudley but it is a good point from which to start trying to identify the LMS presence in Dudley. The low level line was the South Staffordshire Railways line that first reached Dudley in 1850. The high level "Stour Valley" line passes through the northernmost corner of the County Borough of Dudley between Bloomfield and Coseley.
(Paul Dorney)

Left: A two-car Park Royal DMU forms the 4.18.pm Dudley - Walsall train on 25th July 1959, seen here approaching Dudley Port Low Level on 25th July 1959. On the left is the empty stock siding, and the loading shed used by the Palethorpes' Sausage traffic. On the far right is the embankment of the double track spur from Dudley Port High Level down to Sedgeley Junction. On the skyline is Dudley Castle and Castle Hill. The area on the right has now considerably changed as new houses have been built on the site of the allotments and the embankment of the Dudley Port High Level link has been flattened. Michael Mensing)

Left: Branch line and connecting line services operated by auto-trains, or "push-pull" trains, have often earned a nickname among passengers and railwaymen. In Dudley's case we have "The Dasher" and "The Dodger". Sometimes the terms seem to have been used indiscriminately, but generally "The Dasher" seems to have been the service between Dudley and Walsall, and "The Dodger" seems to have been the service between Dudley and Dudley Port High Level. The confusion, of course, is quite legitimate, as no doubt "The Dasher" did a turn or two as "The Dodger" between runs to Walsall! Here "The Dodger" descends the "spur" to Sedgeley Junction in the late 1940s. These veteran 2-4-2Ts, designed by Webb and built for the LNWR in the 1890s, soon became extinct after nationalisation.
(Eric Rogers/Lawrence Brownhill)

The South Staffordshire Line Approaches

Right: Ex GWR streamlined diesel railcar W8 on a Birmingham Snow Hill - Dudley train approaches Sedgeley Junction in the 1950s. On the right is the Palethorpe's Siding, and in the background is the "Stour Valley" line from Birmingham New Street to Wolverhampton High Level, with Dudley Port High Level on the right and Dudley Port Junction Signal Box on the left. The railcar has not stopped at Dudley Port Low Level as BR Western Region continued the GWR policy of passing through the LMS station. (The late Ted Higgs)

Below: Sedgeley Junction Signal Box, of standard LNWR design, at the junction of the Walsall - Dudley "South Staffs" line and the double track spur round to Dudley Port High Level. The box was destroyed by fire on 20th September 1964, shortly after becoming redundant. The wall on the left still stands! Note: the wooden nameboard clearly shows that the railway spelt Sedgley with an extra 'e', although on railways maps it is usually shown with the more conventional spelling. (Nigel Hazlewood)

Above right: From Sedgeley Junction a long goods loop extended up to Dudley itself, and it is seen clearly here on the right of train no.1T49 - an Ambergate - Dudley Special bringing visitors to the Zoo on Whit Monday 17th May 1964. Ex LMS "Jubilee" class 4-6-0, 45579, "Punjab" is passing the ex LNWR yard on the left before passing under the Tipton Road and into Dudley Station. Note the overbridge in the background that once carried a narrow gauge colliery tramway. (Paul Dorney)

Right: Two class 20 locomotives, 20 084 and 20 188 approach Dudley with the Corby - Brierley Hill "tube" train on 28th August 1984. The goods loop and the signal gantry have disappeared, but part of the brickwork of the colliery tramway bridge still exists and the site of the ex LNWR goods yard sidings have been taken over by part of the late Joe Ashmore's amazing scrap yard ventures. Goods trains would, in steam days, generally have to be "banked" up the hill from Great Bridge to Dudley. (Ned Williams)

Southern Approaches

Left: Ex GWR class 94xx 0-6-0PT, 8498, approaches Brettell Lane, and enters the area covered by this book, with the 5.27.pm Stourbridge Junction - Wolverhampton LL local train on Whit Monday 11th June 1962. Although the landscape beyond the goods yard looks fairly rural this area was heavily worked by brick fields, and later overturned by open cast extraction of coal, during the early 1970s. (Michael Mensing)

Left: Ex GWR class 51xx 2-6-2T, 4140, enters Brettell Lane station with the 1.55. pm. Stourbridge Junction - Wolverhampton LL stopping train on Saturday 21st. July 1962 - a week before the service was withdrawn. From 1925 to 1932 it was also possible to travel by passenger train from Brettell Lane to Wolverhampton via the Wombourn line. (Ron Hartshorne)

Below: Just north of Brettell Lane was Kingswinford Junction, first brought into use as a junction in 1858 with the opening of the OWWR branch to Bromley Basin. The branch was extended to Shut End, Oak Farm and Askew Bridge - latterly becoming the southern end of the line to Wolverhampton via Wombourn. (see "The Railway to Wombourn", Uralia Press, 1986.) Kingswinford Junction South Signal Box, seen in this picture, was opened in 1916, and re-framed in 1924 in anticipation of the opening of the Wombourn line. Class 45 locomotive, 45 034, is seen here coming off the branch with trip working T42 from Pensnett on 18th July 1985, as Signalman John James approaches the locomotive to collect the single line token. In the background is Moor Lane Yard, and on the right tracks have just been lifted that formed sidings to serve Messrs. Marsh & Baxter of Brierley Hill. (Paul Dorney)

Brierley Hill

Above: Class 37 locomotive, 37 884, "Gartcosh", leaves Brierley Hill Steel Terminal, Moor Lane, as light engine to Bescot, on 19th March 1993 - the last day the line from Bescot to Round Oak via Dudley was in use. The Pensnett branch curves away to the left just outside the picture. (Ned Williams)

Right: Ex GWR class 51xx 2-6-2T, 4179, arrives at Brierley Hill Station with the 6.20. pm. Worcester - Wolverhampton LL local stopping train on 26th August 1961. In the distance, behind the rear coach, it is possible to see Kingswinford Junction North Signal Box. Brierley Hill had no signal box, and the only siding was into the parcels bay on the up side at the Dudley end of the station (see next page) - access to the siding was controlled from a ground fame, which in turn was controlled from Round Oak South Signal Box. (Michael Mensing)

Right: Ex GWR "Manor" class 4-6-0, 7806, "Cockington Manor" calls at Brierley Hill with a southbound local stopping train from Wolverhampton on 21st January 1961. Brierley Hill station was opened on 1st December 1858, the original OWWR station serving the Brierley Hill area being at Round Oak. The footbridge was added in 1878. Note, the down platform on the left, carries a new enamel station name board, while the up platform still carries its GWR style board with wooden letters. Passenger services ceased at the end of July 1962, but parcels traffic continued to be handled until January 1967. The site was cleared in 1968. (John Dew)

Left: Ex GWR class 28xx 2-8-0, 2817, passes the northern end of the Moor Lane Goods Yard on 8th May 1957. This view, from the Moor Lane bridge shows the Stevens & Williams Glassworks which are still there today. The yard, on the right of the picture, was re-modelled in the 1960s, and re-opened on 31st May 1965 as the Brierley Hill Steel Terminal. (John Dew)

Left: Ex GWR class 57xx 0-6-0PT, 9733, passes Brierley Hill Station with a southbound freight on 26th August 1961. The town of Brierley Hill rises behind the station on the right. (Michael Mensing)

Below: Ex GWR class 43xx 2-6-0, 6349, pulls away from Brierley Hill with a northbound local train for Dudley and Wolverhampton on 2nd May 1957. To the left of the train is the covered goods platform used for dispatching Marsh & Baxter's products as parcels traffic. During the morning an "up" Worcester bound train would drop a van into this bay, during the day it would be loaded, and at 4.26. pm the Wolverhampton - Paddington train would call at Brierley Hill, back into the siding and collect the van. What went on here, and at the station itself, is told by Stan Hill in "The Blackcountryman" Vol.14 No.1. Winter 1981). (P.J.Shoesmith)

Round Oak

Right: An ex GWR "Prairie" enters Round Oak from the south with a local train for Wolverhampton on 28th April 1962. This picture was taken from the footbridge c;learly seen in the picture below. (John Dew)

Right: An ex GWR class 57xx 0-6-0PT, 4696, runs bunker-first into Round Oak with a local stopping train heading towards Stourbridge Junction on 28th April 1962. Looking north, through the footbridge and the road bridge carrying the Brierley Hill - Dudley road it is possible to make out Round Oak South Signal Box. (John Dew)

Right: A 3-car WR DMU forms the 5.35.pm Birmingham Snow Hill - Dudley - Brettell Lane train, passing Round Oak South Signal Box and approaching Round Oak station on Whit Monday 11th June 1962. Note the water column, Round Oak Steel Works on the right, and the buildling which has become the Round Oak Rail Terminal in the distance, and Netherton Church on the skyline. The Pensnett Railway's crossing can just be seen beyond the signal box.

(Michael Mensing)

Round Oak North

Left: An impressive train of bogie and four wheel grain wagons sets out from Round Oak Rail Terminal on 29th April 1986 - removing part of the legendary grain mountain stored in the ex-bar finishing mill building. Class 20s, 20 056 and 20 117 head the train, with class 31, 31 161, is banking at the rear. The train is about to cross the bridge carrying Lord Wards Canal on its way round to the Wallows. A typical Black Country scene looking out to the greenery and mystery of Wychbury Hill.
(Brian Robbins)

Left: A view looking south from Round Oak North Signal Box as ex LMS class 5 4-6-0, 44829 climbs towards Dudley with the Tavistock - Crewe Goods, which includes a number of tarpaulin-covered wagons of china clay. This photograph was taken in 1965 or 1966 after this train had been diverted via Dudley after the closure of its former path over the Wombourn Branch. At the rear of the train, just in front of the outline of Round Oak Steel Works, it is possible to see smoke and steam rising from the banker. On the left is Lord Ward's canal - this stretch still water-filled despite being cut off from the Dudley Canal at Parkhead.
(John Harris)

Below: BR Standard class 2 2-6-0, 78008, brings the 6.05.pm Wolverhampton LL - Stourbridge Junction train past the site of Woodside Station on Whit Monday 11th June 1962, with the Rowley Hills on the skyline. The station opened as "Harts Hill & Woodside" on 1st April 1895 and was closed as from 1st January 1917.
(Michael Mensing)

Above: Looking towards Dudley, with the spire of Top Church on the skyline, class 20 locomotive 20 021 takes a Bescot - Stourbridge Junction permanent way train on its way towards Round Oak, having just crossed the Parkhead Viaduct, on 6th February 1987. (Paul Dorney)

Right: Class 56xx 0-6-2T, 5659, crosses Parkhead Viaduct on 23rd April 1963, looking back towards the point from which the above photograph was taken. (Richard Taylor)

Below: One of the best views of the southern face of Parkhead viaduct was obtained from Peartree Lane (a typical Black Country name for a road that served a totally industrialised environment). From the Peartree Lane canal bridge, class 47 locomotive, 47 310, is seen returning to Bescot with the Brierley Hill trip working on 15th March 1993 - four days before closure of the line. Note the canal signpost, restored locks, and attractive lock-side cottage. (Ned Williams)

Parkhead Viaduct

Climbing towards Dudley, between Round Oak North Box and Blowers Green Sidings, the OWWR line crossed an impressive viaduct traversing a valley full of canals. The canals are converging on the southern approach to the Dudley Canal Tunnel (opened 1792). The viaduct was originally of wooden construction, and it is believed that the original wooden viaduct is "buried" inside its brick-built successor of the 1880s. Other OWWR wooden viaducts were replaced by GWR improvements of that period at Stambermill and just south of Brettell Lane. Problems of maintaining the viaduct in the light of relatively little use may have been a contribution to the decision to close the line between Bescot and Round Oak in 1993.

Left: Class 25 , no. 25 297 , crosses Parkhead Viaduct on 22nd May 1985 with a northbound train. South of Dudley Canal Tunnel the waterway branches in all directions: a short branch to Grazebrook's Netherton Ironworks, a line to the Lapal Tunnel and the Worcester & Birmingham Canal at Selly Oak, the main line through the centre of the picture to the Stourbrdge Canal at The Delph, and Lord Ward's Canal, seen in a "filled in" state passing beneath a bridge to the left of the picture, which passed under the viaduct and paralleled the railway until passing under it again and terminating at The Wallows. (Ned Williams)

Left: Class 47, 47 279 crosses Parkhead Viaduct on 10th March 1993, not long before the line's closure, with "Cargo Rail" wagons from the Pensnett Branch - returning to Bescot. (Paul Dorney)

Left: Blowers Green sidings seen from the overbridge carrying the Dudley - Netherton - Old Hill road at Cinder Bank. The signal box controlling the southern end of the sidings was on the other side of this bridge, behind the photographer. The engine shed of Messrs Grazbrook's railway was to the right of the timber yard on the right, and their railway joined the yard on the right in the middle distance. On the skyline it is possible to see Dudley Gas Works above the point where the railway plunged into Dudley Tunnel, and the chimney at the CWS National Works at Dixons Green. (Viv Morgan)

Blowers Green Junction

Above: 0-6-0PT 6434 propels the autocoach, W254W, past Blowers Green Junction and heads for the Bumble Hole line to Old Hill on 12th June 1964 - the evening before the service was withdrawn. The overbridge in front of the train provided access to the South Staffordshire Wagon Co.'s works, and Netherton church tower can be seen on the skyline. (P.J.Shoesmith)

Below: Class 57xx 0-6-0PT 3607 passes Blowers Green Junction Signal Box with a local trip working returning to Oxley Sidings in the early 1960s. The south west of the Black Country disappears beyond into the haze, but on the original photograph it is possible to see the five chimneys of the open hearth shop at Round Oak Steel Works. (John Harris)

Above: The front and back of Blowers Green junction Signal Box - on the left with the West Midland line tracks in the foreground, on the right seen from the line to Old Hill.
Left: Removing the junction at Blowers Green, seen from the lines to Old Hill. (John Harris)

Left: Class 57xx 0-6-0PT, 3745, brings empty stock, ex Old Hill line, through Blowers Green Station on Whit Monday 11th June 1962. The OWWR opened a station called "Netherton" in 1852 when their line opened to Dudley. When the line to Old Hill opened on 1st March 1878 the original "Netherton" station was replaced with this new station just north of the junction, called "Dudley Southside & Netherton". Access was originally at the tunnel end of the station and although the facilities were considered superior to those at Dudley itself, the local townsfolk disliked the steep descent into the cutting to reach the station. This problem was eventually overcome when access, and a new booking office, were provided at the New Road end of the station. It was renamed "Blowers Green" in August 1921, and closed at the end of July 1962. (Michael Mensing)

The Southern End of Dudley Tunnel

Right: Ex GWR "Grange" class 4-6-0, 6876, "Kingsland Grange" passes the site of Blowers Green Station tender first about 1964 in a picture that illustrates how the gas works dominated the townscape above the southern portal of Dudley Tunnel.

(John Harris)

Right: On 30th August 1992 the "Open Day" at Bescot Yard included among its attractions, three special passenger trains from Bescot over to Dudley via the South Staffordshire line, and down the West Midland line to the Pensnett Branch. The trains carried headboards, "The Pensnett Knocker" and "the Bilston Knob", the latter being a reference to the fact that the trains also traversed the line from Wednesbury to a point just south of Bilston. Due to the number of reversals involved the trains had locomotives at both ends of the train. In this picture, 31 217 and 31 128 bring the train through the site of Blowers Green Station, with 60 083 on the other end of the train - still in Dudley Tunnel. The gas works has vanished from the skyline and the site of the station is increasingly "green".

(Paul Dorney)

Right: "Grange" class 4-6-0, 6856, "Stowe Grange" bursts from the southern portal of Dudley Tunnel in the early 1960s. The tunnel was 949 yards in length.

(John Harris)

The Bumble Hole Line.

The railway from Dudley to Old Hill was authorised by a West Midland Railway Act of 1862, and was part of a scheme to link Dudley with Halesowen, crossing the Stourbridge Railway at Old Hill. Ten years later the GWR had to renew the legal powers to build the line as so little progress had been made. The route traversed an area riddled with uncharted coal pits, and was suffering a recession in the local hardware trade. The line eventually opened on 1st March 1878, providing the long-awaited link between Dudley and Halesowen, and alternative route between Dudley and Birmingham. There was one intermediate station - at Windmill End - just outside the area covered by this book. The area north of Windmill End, dominated by old pit workings, canals and their basins, and flooded "crowning-ins", was known as the "Bumble Hole".

Left: 0-6-0PT 6434 stands at platform 1, Dudley Station, having arrived with the 7.00. pm auto train from Old Hill, on Friday 12th June 1964 - the day before the line's last regular passenger trains. In latter years the service only operated at morning and evening "peak" times, plus the mid-day Saturday workings - hence the few photographers who recorded the final days of the Bumble Hole service tended to photograph the same trains.

(George Bennett)

Left: The signal announces access to the Bumble Hole line is clear for 0-6-0PT 6434 on 12 June 1964 propelling its auto-train through the site of Blowers Green Station en route from Dudley to Old Hill. This picture was taken on the day before the service ceased, but, as can be seen, Blowers Green Station had already disappeared. When the Stourbridge Junction - Wolverhampton service was withdrawn at the end of July 1962, it was hoped that Blowers Green would continue to be served by the Dudley - Old Hill trains, but BR refused to consider the idea, and Blowers Green closed even though the Bumble Hole trains continued to pass through it.

(P.J.Shoesmith)

Left: Class 51xx 2-6-2T, 4111, takes the curve on to the Bumble Hole line immediately south of Blowers Green Junction on Sunday 23rd September 1956, with a local Wolverhampton LL - Birmingham Snow Hill train that has been diverted from its usual path via Bilston, Wednesbury, West Bromwich etc due to engineering works near Priestfield. In the background are the sidings serving the wagon repair works of the South Staffordshire Wagon Co., and on the skyline, to the right it is possible to see the chimney at Hanson's Brewery and the spire of Top Church. The skyline on the left features the trees that bordered the playing field of the Gilbert Claughton Grammar School.

(Michael Mensing)

Above left: Windmill End Junction Signal Box stood at the point where the branch to Withymoor Basin, also known as "Netherton Goods", diverged from the Bumble Hole line, just south of Baptist End Halt. The branch opened on 10th March 1879 - the year after the Bumble Hole line itself had opened. The branch, which had served irnworks as well as the canal basin, was less than a mile in length, and closed on 5th July 1965. (Edgar Rumble)

Above Right: A BR single-unit diesel railcar passes Windmill End Junction and approaches Baptist End Halt on 31st August 1962. The halts had been "modernised" in the 1950s and some trains on the line were operated by these modern railcars, but right until the end, in June 1964, some trains were still steam operated at a time when virtually every other local passenger service was dieselised. (P.J.Shoesmith)

Below: This picture of Withymoor Basin/Netherton Goods was taken from the footbridge in Northfield Road, Netherton, which the branch crossed on the level at the throat of the yard. The frequency of trains on the branch and the position of the level crossing in relation to the yard presumably necessitated the footbridge. Class 57xx 0-6-0PT no.3605 pauses in the yard between shunting and trip working sometime in 1963. (Ned Williams)

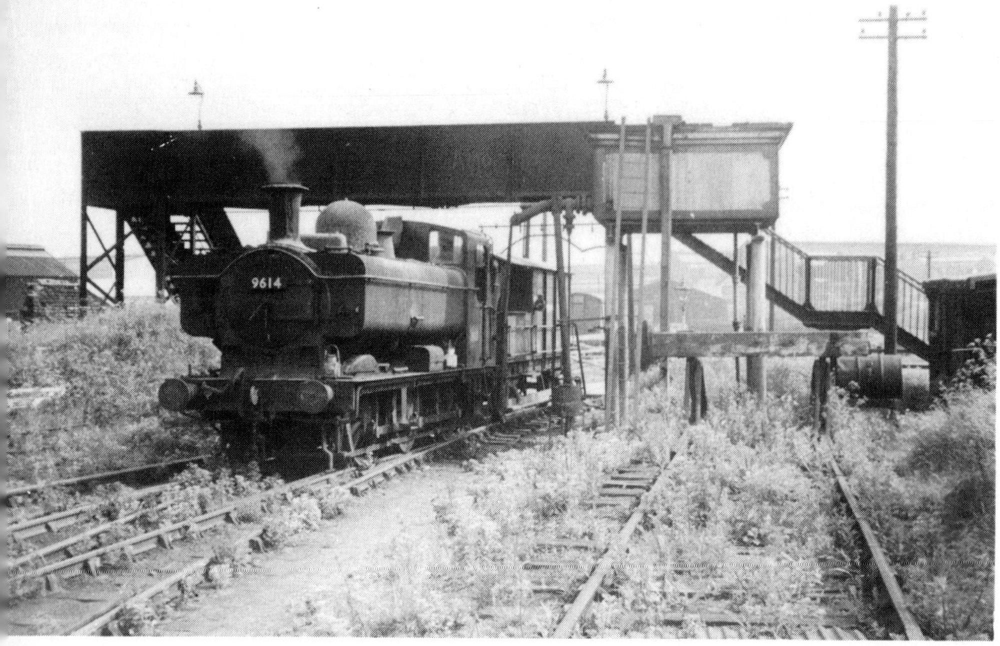

Left: Ex.GWR class 57xx 0-6-0PT, 9614, has just crossed the Northfield Road Level Crossing on the Netherton Goods Branch, and has drawn alongside the water tank on 10th June 1965. The branch closed a few weeks later on 5th July - perhaps accounting for the weedy condition of the track. In the background is the footbridge from which the picture on the previous page was taken. The water tank was "preserved", and is now to be found at Eardington on the Severn Valley Railway. (Paul Dorney)

Left: The Bumble Hole Line remained open for through goods trains after the cessation of the passenger service in June 1964, and the closure of the goods only line from Windmill End Junction to Netherton Goods the following year. Total closure came on 1st January 1968. During 1965 and 1966 the through freight traffic was worked by large engines such as the Standard 9F 2-10-0s, as seen here. No. 92228 leaves Blowers Green Junction and takes the curve towards Baptist End Halt with the "ironstone empties" running from Bilston Steelworks back to Banbury. 9F locomotives also worked the trains from the Rowley Regis Oil Depot over the branch. On the left is the old Breeze Block factory. (John Harris)

Left: This picture is included as it provides a good view of the "driving end" of auto-trailer W254W - taken while waiting in the bay at Dudley on 28th December 1963. 0-6-0PT no. 6424 is on the other end of the train and is about to leave with the trailer as the 12.26. Saturdays Only train to Old Hill. Once it was announced that closure would take place in the following June, this train and its return working provided the only "middle of the day" photographic opportunity for recording the line's existence. The journey was regularly undertaken in fog! (Ron Moss)

The Earl of Dudley's Railways

Historical Introduction

A glance at the map on page 4 reveals that the mileage of private industrial railway within the Dudley area far exceeded the mileage of public "common carrier" railway, and therefore no survey of "The Railways of Dudley" is complete without a look at this complex, ever changing, network of industrial lines. They were "industrial" lines in the sense that they came into existence primarily to serve the industry and mining that developed in the south western corner of the Black Country during the nineteenth century. A good deal of such railway, but not all, belonged to the Earl of Dudley. (For convenience this is the name used to describe the "proprietor" of the Dudley Estate, and the head of the Ward family, although the "Earldom" became extinct in 1833, and was re-created in 1860!)

The term "Earl of Dudley's Railways" is used to provide an umbrella under which we can consider the original Kingswinford Railway or Shut End Railway, the later Pensnett Railway, a term then used to describe the combined system, and the railways that served the immediate vicinity of the steelworks at Round Oak, known locally as, "The Earl's". The railway's history has been described in the late W.K.V. Gale's book, "The History of the Pensnett Railway". (Goose, 1975.)

The south west corner of the Black Country was rich in mineral resources but developed later than the eastern half of the Black Country as it was relatively inaccessible. The Staffordshire and Worcestershire Canal opened in 1772 but passed well to the west of the area concerned. The Stourbridge Canal opened in 1779 to the Delph at Brierley Hill, and to the Fens of Pensnett Chase, where reservoirs would provide a water supply. The Stourbridge Extension Canal, bringing the waterway right into the area concerned was not authorised until as late as 1837, by which time a railway had arrived on the scene.

James Foster, a Stourbridge iron master, and the Earl of Dudley agreed to build a railway from the Shut End area to the the Staffs & Worcs Canal at Ashwood Basin, a distance of nearly three miles. After agreement was reached in 1827, the basin at Ashwood was built to receive outgoing coal, and a quarter of a mile long railway incline was built from there to the "main line" of the Shut End Railway which ran across country, past the village of Kingswinford and to the foot of another incline, known as "Foster's Incline", that lifted the line to its eastern terminus near an area we would now call Pensnett.

On the 2nd June 1829 the steam locomotive, "Agenoria", proudly opened the railway by hauling eight "carriages", carrying three hundred and sixty passengers, plus four wagons of coal, along the central "main line" section of the railway. As a steam locomotive operated standard gauge railway it was one of the pioneers of such transport, but remained less known to the outside world than its contempories because of its isolation, and because it was very much a private concern. In fact the railway, and its successors, were not built via the usual public process of Parliamentary authorisation - they were simply built on private land, much of which belonged to the Earl of Dudley, under powers the family had acquired under the local Enclosure acts.

"Agenoria" worked coal traffic over the Shut End Railway, also known as the Kingswinford Railway, in complete isolation from any other standard gauge railway until 1865. In 1885 W.O.Foster donated the locomotive to the Science Museum, thus ensuring its survival to the present day. Sidings and connecting tramroads were added and subtracted as pits came into use and were abandoned in the area at the Kingswinford end of the line. A junction was later installed at the foot of "Foster's Incline" to serve Bradley's Ironworks, which grew into the major industrial concern in the Shut End area, obliterating small pits and forges, and becoming an "integrated" works - using coal and ironstone mined "on the spot", producing an outward flow of pig iron, and later finished iron.

There were also small pits developing in the area between Barrow Hill and the Dudley-Himley turnpike road. It was considered, during the 1840s, that it would be useful to link these by rail with the Level New Furnaces established by the Dudley Canal, near Round Oak, just north of Brierley Hill. This led to the building of the Pensnett Railway, which grew in importance with subsequent building of the Round Oak Ironworks, in the 1850s. The Pensnett Railway opened in 1846 and, as first built, ran from just north of Barrow Hill, up the 1 in 25 Barrow Hill Incline then across the Fens on a high embankment stretching from Pensnett to The Wallows, where it served a wharf built at the end of Lord Ward's Canal, and then down another incline to the Level New Furnaces.

One interesting point is that an engine driver was engaged in 1846, indicating that the line was locomotive worked from the start, but also interesting in that his name was Charles Mace, and he had just worked on the construction of the OWWR. He was followed by son William, and then by grandson Leonard, who by the 1940s was the line's traffic foreman.

In the 1850s the Oxford Worcester &

Below: The late Keith Gale took this picture from the top of the Tipsyford Incline in July 1950 - looking down to the point where the Earl of Dudley's line passed under the Pedmore Road, close to the Robin Hood pub. The trees of Saltwells Wood are still there today, concealing stories of mining, coppicing, and a long lost "spa", but nearly all trace of the incline has vanished. A dramatic view of "Lady Morveth" ascending the Tipsyford Incline's 1 in 4 grade, assisted on the rope and chain, is to be found on page 11 of George Chatham's "Steam at round Oak" (Halmar, 1967)

Below: A "wagon repair" card used on the Pensnett Railway.

Wolverhampton Railway (OWWR) made its way northwards from Stourbridge, through Brierley Hill, and on to Dudley. At Round Oak the OWWR and the Pensnett Railway had to cross one another on the level. One local legend tells that the PR had priority over the OWWR because it was there first but this has no foundation in fact. The crossing was always controlled by the main line railway, was re-sited in 1871, and was only finally removed in the 1980s!

The Pensnett Railway began to expand in the 1850s, firstly into the Saltwells area, then to Primrose Basin, south of Netherton, on to Old Hill, and finally down to Cradley Heath. From 1855 onwards the PR began to play a part in providing internal rail facilities within the new Ironworks, as well as feeding it with coal and ironstone from outside.

At Shut End the transport situation was altered by the northward extension of the Bromley Basin Branch of the onetime OWWR. By the 1860s this had reached Oak Farm which brought it into close proximity to the northern end of the PR. Bradley & Foster had purchased their first steam locomotive in 1865 and were interested in seeing improvements made to the Shut End Railway/Kingswinford Railway. In 1865 the two systems were linked by a line from Himley Colliery No3 at the northern end of the PR to the Kingswinford Railway's spur to the Stallings Farm area. A decade later the PR was linked to the GWR close to Askew Bridge. (All this is explained in more detail in Gale's book and "The Railway to Wombourn" - Uralia Press 1986.)

Another branch of the PR took it across the Old Park towards Dudley where the line terminated at a land sale wharf at Wellington Road. This had also been added in 1865. In 1870 a short branch was put in to serve the Dawley Brook gasworks at Kingswinford. In 1874 the Cradley Heath line was extended across the main road to join the "Stourbridge Extension" line of the GWR. There were even one or two "detached" parts of the Earl of Dudley's railway system. The most notable was the line from Dudley Station to the Earl's Castle Mill Works.

In the 1870s the railway employed eleven engines on almost forty miles of track. In 1876 it employed a total of 152 men and boys. This was the hey-day of the system, and lasted until the decline of the local iron trade in the 1880s. Round Oak switched to the manufacture of steel, but used ore imported from other areas. Local ironstone deposits were virtually exhausted anyway. Bradley & Fosters Ironworks closed but the site was worked for other products and Guy Pitt & Co, explored the remaining mineral interests in the area. The work of the PR shifted from its sprawling network to closer ties with Round Oak Steel Works.

As the small pits found in the Himley and Saltwells coalfields were worked out, the search began for better supplies of coal from new areas, even deep below ground on the other side of the Boundary Fault. Exploraratory borings were made at Baggeridge Wood, near the Earl's home at Himley Hall, at the end of the nineteenth century. Baggeridge Colliery eventually came into production in 1912. The GWR helped build a branch from Askew Bridge up to the colliery, replacing an earlier narrow gauge tramway, and the new line, built to GWR standards became part of the PR. The PR also acquired new traffic with the opening of the Gibbons Railway from near Barrow Hill to Gibbons' Dibdale works. This line had opened in 1899.

An interesting feature of the PR's twentieth century existence was the passenger service provided every year from 1929 to 1937 for the Himley Fetes. Passengers joined the train at The Wallows, using temporary wooden platforms, and travelled over the Fens Pool embankment, down the Barrow Hill Incline, round to Askew Bridge and the spur onto the Baggeridge Line. They disembarked at another temporary wooden platform at "High Arcal" - the point where the Baggeridge line passed through the corner of the Himley Estate. It seems that the PR carried over 60,000 passengers between 1929 and 1937 at the time of the Fetes.

After the Second World War the outer tentacles of the PR fell into disuse. The Saltwells lines were lifted in the early 1950s. Ashwood Basin fell into disuse towards the end of 1953 when Baggeridge coal ceased being dispatched to Stourport power station via the canal. Traffic to Dawley Brook ceased a couple of years later. Wellington Road Wharf appears to have closed in the mid 1950s. Traffic on the Baggeridge line was complicated by the nationalisation of the coal industry, and then the nationalisation of the steel industry, After the latter, the NCB provided its own engines for working between Baggeridge and Askew Bridge, at which point it handed over the coal wagons to BR or to the PR.The forward movement of coal from Askew Bridge to the steelworks ceased in 1966. (The NCB's delivery of coal to BR via Baggeridge Junction ceased two years later when the pit closed.)

New finishing mills at the Old Level led to some rearranging of the PR in that area in the 1950s - resulting in the provision of a new level crossing over Level Street about 1939. The last signs of the crossing survived long enough to disappear under the redevelopment of the Merry Hill and Waterfront areas.

Dieselisation came to the Pensnett Railway in 1963 and from the mid 1960s onwards the line's diesel fleet almost exclusively served Round Oak Steelworks until its closure in 1982. The entire diesel locomotive fleet remained "in store" at Round Oak while the steelworks went through its painful demolition process. This itself did not begin for over a year as there was no buyer for the closed works. Eventually the Richardson Brothers stepped in, following some re-alignment of the boundaries of the Dudley Enterprise Zone to include the "backyard" of the steelworks. The development of the Merry Hill Centre and the Waterfront have gradually removed the remains of the steelworks and its railway system. The Wallows, the headquarters of the PR, disappeared into a new industrial estate, and the former bar finishing mill made the amazing transformation into a Rail Terminal and Store, thus providing a new home for the railway's diesel locomotives. This came into use gradually amidst local rumours that European "grain mountains" were being stored there, and then was opened "officially" on 3rd September 1986 to accept delivery of coils of rolled steel.

In 1994 we are left with a "rump" of "main line" railway line extending north from Stourbridge Junction to Round Oak, where a remnant of the PR - the old Earl of Dudley's railway system, provides a few realigned sidings into the new Rail Terminal. A few ex PR diesel locomotives are still at work. Will they make the 21st Century?

Left: "Brandon", an 0-4-0 tender engine supplied to the Earl of Dudley's railway by Manning Wardle in 1859 (their works number 6). It seems that the locomotives constructed at Castle Mill Works followed Manning Wardle/E.B.Wilson practice, and may have been constructed from parts supplied by them.

(Collection of Keith Gale)

Above: The classic view of steam at Round Oak: a Barclay 0-4-0ST and slag-tipping wagon crosses Level Street on 2nd May 1959. This view, from the back of Round Oak Steel Works looks out across coal-bearing "countryside" to the hill on which Netherton church stands. The "Enterprise Zone" and the Merry Hill Centre have since added their mark to this landscape, but there are also ancient pastures preserved by the Saltwells Nature Reserve, new 20th century canal-scapes, a sea-going life boat and a mono-rail all helping maintain Dudley's reputation for variety and surprises.
(P.J.Shoesmith)

Right: Yorkshire Engine Co. 0-4-0 diesel no.10 (2883 of 1963) - the last of the fleet - approaches the original crossing on Level Street from the finishing mills in the mid 1960s. Both level crossings across Level Street were given lifting barriers and austere crossing control cabins about 1960. Originally this line had provided access to the "southern" half of the Earl of Dudley's railway system via the Tipsyford Incline.
(Viv Morgan)

Right: "Peter" (Andrew Barclay, 0-6-0ST 1965 Of 1929) marshals the four wheel coaches hired from the GWR for use on the Himley Fete passenger train, seen here at the Wallows. (The same train is seen at Himley on page 67)
(Collection of Keith Gale)

A Visit to the Earl of Dudley's Railway in 1910.

Early in 1910 the Earl of Dudley's railway system was visited by Mr.T.R.Perkins - a gentleman who was setting out to travel over every mile of Britain's railways, recording information and taking photographs. He wrote about his visit in the May and June 1910 issues of "The Locomotive", and, of course, this gives us a first hand description of the line in its heyday.

He was motivated by a desire to see the line where "Agenoria", then at the Science Museum in London, had once performed her daily toil for thirty years. He was not disappointed: ..."*We were surprised and delighted to find that the present day traffic over the celebrated line is worked by a staff of locomotives possessing an interest little inferior to that of "Agenoria" itself.*"

Mr.Perkins and his companion were shown round the system by the Manager - a Mr.Mantle - who met them at Ashwood Basin. Unfortunately Mr.Mantle died before the account of the visit appeared in print, but he was obviously very helpful to the visitors as their account reveals:

"At the foot of the incline, the locomotive 'Queen', which Mr.Mantle had place at our disposal for the trip, awaited us, and before mounting the footplate, we both took the opportunity of inspecting this most interesting engine - an 0-6-0 side tank built by Manning Wardle in 1865, which is in practically original condition, with fine fluted copper dome on square setting - it remains an excellent example of the locomotive practice of the 1880s."

They set off from Ashwood and headed eastwards, crossing the Wolverhampton - Worcester Road on the level at Wall Heath, and commenting on the fact that they then crossed the Wolverhampton - Stourbridge road, at Kingswinford, on a girder bridge with brick abutments. The bridge has entirely disappeared today but it is commemorated in the name of the nearby Bridge Inn.

"A few hundred yards beyond this bridge the present main line diverges from the original Shutt End Railway by a sharp curve to the left, the remaining portion of the old line now being chiefly used as a means of access to Messrs Foster's colliery, and worked by their engines. The (Shutt End) incline is almost entirely disused.

The semi-circular detour which the main line makes between Kingswinford and Pensnett enables it to touch several collieries in the Himley district. Two junctions, some half a mile apart, afford connection with a mineral branch of the GWR extending towards the new colliery in Baggeridge Wood. The Baggeridge extension has only been completed within the last two years."

The visitors then reach the foot of the Barrow Hill Incline - a 1 in 25 rope worked incline - now turned into a public footpath. 'Queen' was moved to the rear of the train of wagons and assisted the stationary engine in moving them to the top of the incline at the point where the line passed under Pensnett Road. Mr.Perkins observed the loco shed at the foot of the incline.

In the second part of the article the rest of the journey was described - travelling on 'Queen's" footplate across the Fens Pools embankment where they noticed some primitive signalling in use, and approaching Round Oak - the centre of the railway system at The Wallows. They inspected the marshalling yards, running sheds and offices and noted that light repairs were carried out there, while heavy repairs were carried out at the Castle Mill Works, just north of Dudley Station. This meant the Earl's engines had to be hauled "dead" over the GWR's West Midland line to and from the Castle Mill works. It is interesting to note that Mr.Perkins observed the branch extending northwards from The Wallows towards Dudley, but decided not to travel over it as it was of little interest! (Today, it is that line that is more difficult for us to imagine, while the line down Barrow Hill can be "imagined" if only because the route still exists.)

Mr.Mantle went out of his way to enable Mr.Perkins to inspect all the locomotive stock of the railway, which included five locomotives that still resembled their 1850s appearance. Mr.Perkins explained to the readers that the engines were being modernised and rebuilt as they passed through the Castle Mill works, and were emerging with modern saddle tanks and Belpaire fireboxes. He observed 'Countess', of 1857, as being the most primitive locomotive still in use.

'Victory', originally Manning Wardle 94 of 1863 had been rebuilt in 1896 and others had been rebuilt in the years leading up to Mr.Perkins' visit: 'Edward VII" in 1902, 'Alexandra' in 1904, 'Dudley' in 1906, and 'Alma' in 1908. It seemed that 'Round Oak ' was being rebuilt at the time of his visit. He also saw four "modern" locomotives before continuing on his tour.

They took the line that crossed the GWR on the level and entered the world of the Earl of Dudley's Round Oak Ironworks, and then down the rope-worked incline to Saltwells Junction, where the lines diverged again. Whether he travelled right down through Mushroom Green to the GWR yard at Cradley Heath is not clear as he was more concerned with the locomotives he had seen than the geography of the area through which he travelled. The articles are well-illustrated with the photographs he took of the system's locomotive stock.

Left: "Queen" , the locomotive on which Mr.T.R.Perkins travelled in 1910. "Queen" began life as an 0-6-0T (Manning Wardle 227 of 1867, not "1865" as Mr.Perkins thought.) built for John Bradley & Co. of the shut End Ironworks. She was acquired by the Earl of Dudley's Railway in 1896. It was scrapped about 1926. (Collection of Keith Gale)

Above: "Edward VII" was an 0-4-0ST built at the Earl of Dudley's Castle Mill Works in 1902. It was rebuilt at the Works in 1915 but was scrapped before 1936 when the Earl of Dudley's locomotives became part of the equipment of the newly formed Round Oak Steelworks Ltd. (The maker's plate reads: "Earl of Dudley, Castle Mill Works, 1902, Dudley")
(Collection of the late Keith Gale)

Right: "Prince of Wales", an Andrew Barclay 0-6-0ST (2002 of 1934) which survived until 1962.
(Collection of Jack Reynolds)

Right: "Billy" , an Andrew Barclay 0-4-0ST (1881 of 1925) which survived until the end of steam at Round Oak, and was cut up towards the end of 1963.
(Collection of Jack Reynolds)

Left: Last Day of Steam at the Wallows - at the end of June 1963.

Left to right: Tom Batham (fitter) stands next to Paddy. Billy Holden (Wagon-breaking yard foreman) leans on the smokebox, in front of him is Ted Hamilton (boilersmith), next to Stan Staves (wagon shed foreman). Leaning on the buffer is Charlie Tomkins (loco fitter), and behind him is Les Willis (loco fitter). On the footplate, by the cab, is Alan Manton.
(Collection of Jack Reynolds)

Below: "Lady Rosemary", an 0-6-0ST Peckett (1577 of 1921), scrapped about 1949. (Collection of Jack Reynolds)

Below: "Lady Honor", an Andrew Barclay 0-4-0ST (1998 of 1933), carrying the extra lower buffer beam for pushing the "slag bogies" within the works.
(Collection of Jack Reynolds)

Ends of the line.

Ashwood Basin

Right: The view from the road bridge that crosses the basin, shortly before abandonment of the line to Ashwood. In the far distance are the coal staithes seen in the photograph below. The scene is now transformed by the development of a marina. (Collection of Jack Reynolds)

Right: As well as sidings stretching along both sides of the basin at Ashwood, two tracks ventured on to these wooden staithes to discharge coal into the narrowboats below. These do not seem to have been used after the War. (Keith Gale 1950)

Baggeridge Colliery

Right: Exploring for coal north of the Russells Hall Fault began at the end of the last century as the shallow pits around Shut End became exhausted. The exploration shaft was sunk at Baggeridge, north of the Earl of Dudley's home at Himley Hall in 1898, and led to some interesting railway developments including a narrow gauge "tramway" from the Earl of Dudley's Railway up into Baggeridge Woods. The GWR showed interest in putting the colliery on their railway map, and acted as engineers to the Earl of Dudley for the construction of a line from Askew Bridge to the pit. The actual construction was carried out to GWR specification by the contractors Henry Lovatt Ltd., and was part of the GWR's "Wolverhampton & Bridgnorth" railway scheme which included upgrading the line from Kingswinford Junction to Askew Bridge and Oak Farm. The operation of the pit, which started production in 1912, and the railway remained within the empire of the Earl of Dudley. In this view, taken in the 1920s, one of the new Andrew Barclay tanks is shunting the sidings serving the colliery screens. The pit closed in March 1968. (BCS . Collection)

Left: The bridge conveying the Ashwood Basin line over the Kingswinford - Wolverhampton Road carried the legend, "Buy Baggeridge Coal", but the word "Baggeridge" was painted out during the Second World War, and in 1947 the pit was nationalised anyway, so when this picture was taken in 1950, the exhortation to simply "Buy Coal" was appropriate! The bridge ceased to be used in 1953 when trains of coal from Baggeridge no longer made their way down to Ashwood Basin for canal shipment to Stourport Power Station. On the left was the gas works at Dawley Brook, also served by a siding on the PR. (Keith Gale)

Left: The ungated level crossings on the Earl of Dudley's railway system were guarded by crossing keepers who were provided with brick-built beehive shaped shelters. This one was situated at the point where the Ashwood line crossed Stallings Lane, photographed in 1950. The stone above the door carried the date "1870". Mr.J.Walker was the crossing keeper in 1950. (Keith Gale)

Left: "Lady Morvyth" (Andrew Barclay 0-4-0ST 2054 of 1938) taking water at the supply available at the site of Himley No.8 Pit in April 1950. The 0-4-0STs shunted the yard at Baggeridge Pit at this time, but that duty also included at least one trip down to Ashwood Basin using a direct line that avoided any reversal at Askew Bridge. (Keith Gale)

Askew Bridge (PR)

Right: Looking towards Ashwood, the Pensnett Railway can be seen passing under the northern limits of the Askew Bridge Branch of the GWR, which after 1925 simply became part of the Earl of Dudley's system so that wagons from Baggeridge Colliery could be handed over to the main line company closer to Baggeridge Junction. (See diagram on page 13 of "The Railway to Wombourn", Uralia Press 1986.) The wagons on the Baggeridge Junction - Askew Bridge line seem to include a wagon load of pit props.

(Keith Gale, 1951)

Right: Retreating eastwards from the spot used to take the photograph above, this picture still shows the same overbridge, but the spur to the right of the engine house can now be seen. This spur connected the PR to the Askew Bridge Branch and gave access to the line up to Baggeridge Colliery which curved away round the roofless engine house seen in the distance.

(Tim Shuttleworth, 19/4/52)

Below: "Duchess of Gloucester" (Andrew Barclay 0-6-0ST 2110 of 1941) stands near the point leading to the Askew Bridge/Baggeridge Colliery spur on 19th April 1952, which was obviously the occasion of a railway enthusiasts' visit.

(Tim Shuttleworth)

Barrow Hill Incline

Left: "Queen Elizabeth" and "Lady Morvyth" (Andrew Barclay 0-6-0ST 2044 of 1937, and 0-4-0ST 2054 of 1938, respectively) stand at the foot of Barrow Hill Incline early evening sometime in 1952. "Lady Morvyth" has probably spent the day at Baggeridge Colliery, and "Queen Eilzabeth" has probably been working between the Colliery and the foot of the incline. The picture is taken looking towards the incline and the disused engine shed can be seen on the left. (Tim Shuttleworth)

Left: "Duchess of Gloucester" (Andrew Barclay 0-6-0ST 2110 of 1941) storms up the Barrow Hill Incline on 8th June 1951, propelling seven loaded open wagons of coal. (A W Croughton via Phil Jones)

Left: "Jeremy" (Andrew Barclay 0-6-0ST 1926 of 1927) has almost reached the top of Barrow Hill Incline in this picture, taken on 30th May 1951. The front of the train is just passing under the Pensnett Road. To the left of the photographer is the church yard of St. Mark's Church, Pensnett, and today the incline has been turned into a leafy footpath descending Barrow Hill and providing part of a trackbed walk that could begin at the Wallows and could end in Wolverhampton via the trackbed of the Wombourn line.
(A W Croughton via Phil Jones)

Right: "Jeremy" (Andrew Barclay 0-6-0ST , 1926 of 1927) stands at the crest of the Barrow Hill Incline, just in front of the bridge (or "tunnel") carrying the Pensnett Road over the railway on 30th May 1951. "Jeremy" was the first of the large Barclay 0-6-0STs to be supplied for working the Barrow Hill Incline. Generally an 0-4-0ST was sent to work the yard at Baggeridge Colliery, and the main line was then worked in three sections: Baggeridge Colliery to Askew Bridge, The Barrow Hill Incline, and finally from here to the Wallows. Once the railway had enough 0-6-0STs each of the three sections could be worked by these larger engines.
(A W Croughton via Phil Jones)

Steam at The Wallows

Below: A very atmospheric study of engines resting at the Wallows on 1st June 1951. At the front is "Duchess of Kent" , an Andrew Barclay 0-4-0ST (2007 of 1935), followed by "Jubilee", an Andrew Barclay 0-6-0ST (2012 of 1935). Behind "Jubilee" is the Hippodrome - the maintenance and heavy repair shed built at the same time as Dudley's Hippodrome theatre. It was built to carry out work that had been previously undertaken at the Earl of Dudley's Castle Mill Works.
(A W Croughton via Phil Jones)

Left: "Princess Margaret" (Andrew Barclay 0-4-0ST 2115 of 1942) was among the last of the engines to be scrapped at the end of 1963. This photograph was posed to mark the end of steam at Round Oak, and featured the shunters and controllers working in the Open Hearth Shop area, taken in June 1963.

(Collection of Jack Reynolds)

Left: The "Old Cossing": The Pensnett Railway, having passed under the Dudley - Breierly Hill Road, had to cross the GWR (ex OWWR) mainline on the level before swinging round into the Round Oak Steel Works. Sidings were put in along side the GWR line, and eventually the P.R. crossed eight tracks at this point. As the Earl's line had arrived first the OWWR had to climb to cross the line on the level - rather that the Earl lower his line. This possibly gave rise to the local myth that PR trains had precedence over main line trains in occupying the crossing. The truth is that the crossing was always under the control of the main line signalman. The P.R. was realigned in 1970 when the works was modernised and the "new" crossing remained in situ until 1984. (Keith Gale)

Below: Andrew Barclay 0-4-0ST "Winston" (2116 of 1942) stands with a train of steel tipper wagons at Round Oak on 19th April 1952. The locomotives used on internal steelworks traffic, as opposed to working to the distant parts of the PR, were fitted with an extra lower buffer beam, slotted for coupling to the bogies used for some internal traffic. **(Tim Shuttleworth)**

Right: One of the Andrew Barclay 0-4-0STs nestles alongside the works, close to the five chimneys of the open hearth furnaces. The chimneys were a major landmark in the south west corner of the Black Country. This photograph was taken on 2nd May 1959, and by this time most of the rolling stock carried the letters "PR" - note that the bauxite-coloured wooden open wagons in the foreground are numbered in the 7000s. Behind the locomotive is a rake of steel tipping wagons used for carrying waste material from the works to the tips.
(P.J. Shoesmith)

Right: Yorkshire Engine Co. 0-4-0 diesel locomotive no.1 (2593 of 1955) stands by one of the numerous level crossings within the steel works on 30th May 1980. The short wheel base diesel electric locomotives were able to traverse the sharp curves of the steel works trackwork with the same ease as the Andrew Barclay 0-4-0STs, but were much more powerful, particularly when it came to moving the heavy cauldron wagons of molten metal. (Gordon Nutt)

Right: Yorkshire Engine Co. 0-4-0 diesel locomotive no.3 (2662 of 1957), was photographed on 21st September 1980 on the track that led from the sheds at the Wallows back into the steel works. The main running lines from the works out to the Wallows and beyond are on the left. The bridge carrying the main Brierley Hill - Dudley road separated the Wallows, the operational hub of the railway system, from the steel works itself. The premises of Messrs Westwood & Wright, on the extreme right of the picture had rail access from the Wallows.
(Gordon Nutt)

Above left: The Wallows was very much at the centre of the system, partly because the maintenance facilities were established here (on the left of the picture), but also because wharves were provided alongside Lord Ward's Canal. Coal from the Earl of Dudley's Himley Coalfield was brought to this point over the Pensnett Railway and transhipped to the canal, but there was also incoming traffic in the form of ironstone. When this photograph was taken, on 2nd May 1959, the steel works was consuming vast quantities of scrap iron - carried in the metal-bodied wagons seen beyond the crane. (P.J. Shoesmith)

Above right: The sidings near the Wallows were the home of a steam crane that was rebuilt with a diesel engine during the general process of dieselisation at Round Oak. Here in 1963 Bill Prosser, who had started work at Round Oak in 1921, is seen at the controls.

Left: Andrew Barclay 0-6-0ST "Queen Elizabeth" approaching the Wallows from High Lanes with Michael Hoskison on the footplate on the occasion of one of Messrs Hoskinson and Gale's footplate tours. T.M.Hoskison (Michael's father) was appointed manager of the Level New Furnaces about 1926, and over the years collected information for a book on the Pensnett Railway. He died in 1965, and Keith Gale carried on with the project, publishing the results ten years later.

Left: Keith and the Hoskisons travelled on the footplate of "Queen Elizabeth" up the line to Wellington Road Wharf. On the return trip Keith took this picture from the footplate looking along the train of empties. The shunter is acting "look out" at the far end of the train, as was the custom. We have to be grateful that Keith Gale took it as footplate views from journeys on the Wellington Road branch are not exactly ten a penny! To the left of the train are the houses on Kingswinford Road, Scott's Green, and to the right are the desolate wastes of the "Old Park" on which the Russells Hall Estate has been built. It is just possible to make out the shape of Barrow Hill on the skyline. (Keith Gale - Feb. 1951)

Left: Later in 1951 A.W.Croughton stood at the same location and photographed "Duchess of Gloucester" (Andrew Barclay 2110 of 1941) propelling full coal wagons towards the Wellington Road Wharf on 30th May. Once again the outline of Barrow Hill can be seen on the horizon. This picture can be paired with the picture at the top of page 77. (A W Croughton via Phil Jones)

Above: "Duchess of Gloucester" (Andrew Barclay 0-6-0ST 2110 of 1941) was ten years old when photographed at the Wellington Road Landsale Wharf on 30th May 1951. Beyond the train it is possible to make out the landsale weighbridge office, which carried a plaque bearing the date "1864". Beyond that is the Earl of Dudley's Arms, a Hanson's pub demolished in the 1960s and replaced with a new version on the opposite side of Wellington Road. The wharf appears to have closed soon after this picture was taken and no sign of its existence remains. Few people realise the Earl's railway system came so close to the centre of Dudley .

(A W Croughton via Phil Jones)

Right: The line to Baggeridge Colliery is really geographically beyond the borders of the area covered by this book, and even today would be in South Staffordshire rather than the West Midlands, but it is illustrated here for "completeness".

"Queen Elizabeth" (Andrew Barclay 0-6-0ST 2044 of 1937) is seen here on 8th June 1951, propelling empty wagons back up to the pit. The train has just passed under the Himley Road bridge and the shunter is standing in the front of the first wagon as "look-out" - a common working practice on a line where so many trains were propelled rather than pulled.

(A W Croughton via Phil Jones)

Right: The pre-war passenger trains to the Himley Fetes used the Baggeridge Colliery line, but stopped well short of the pit. It was customary to build a temporary wooden platform, but there it appears that the trains were longer than the platforms!

"Peter" is seen here with a train of the four wheel coaches borrowed for the occasion from the GWR. Temporary bars had to be screwed in place across the windows as clearance was very limited when passing under Pensnett Road, at the top of the Barrow Hill Incline. "Peter" was an Andrew Barclay 0-6-0ST (1965 of 1929).

Collection of the late Keith Gale)

Above: Brake Van no.4 is seen here, at the Wallows, on 19th April 1952. "E D" stood for Earl of Dudley - not "Engineering Department"! The brake van was used on the passenger trains worked before the war to Himley Fetes, and was used as a mess van and road van, but normal everyday traffic over the railway was operated without the use of brake vans. (Tim Shuttleworth)

Left: The Earl of Dudley's Railway generally purchased wagons second hand from the main line railway companies, but wagon repair facilities at the Wallows were extensive, and were capable of wagon building. This photograph was taken in 1950 when the railway operated about 1100 wagons all for its own "internal" use. Generally the wooden bodied seven plank open wagon was most useful, but there was a considerable variety of wagons in use. These two low-sided wagons belonged to the stores department, and carry the letters "R O" and "E D". In later years many wagons carried the letters "P R". (Keith Gale)

Left: Several "private owner" wagons were also worked over the Earl of Dudley's Railway. In the 1930s Constable & Hart processed the steel works slag to produce road metalling material in their works near the foot of the Tipsyford Incline, as the line made for Saltwells. The Earl of Dudley's system ran a few "EDROW" (Earl of Dudley - Round Oak Works) private owner wagons of its own for external use -fetching furnace coke from South Wales, for example. (Keith Gale)

Working at the Wallows

Jack Reynolds

Recorded 16th May 1994

As a child I lived in Brierley Hill and we used to go down to Ashwood on our bikes to swim in the canal. The water was crystal clear, although it was a coal wharf - and that is where I first encountered the Pensnett Railway. The water was beautiful to swim in, and we could dive down and fetch up lumps of coal. We saw the trains because the wharf was in use all the time then. Another childhood encounter with the railway was the times we rode in coal trucks to the Himley fetes. They used to put a guard's van on the train to put the brake on, but as a child it never occurred to me that descending the Barrow Incline in open coal trucks might be dangerous. They used to borrow coaches from the main line and anyone with clean clothes on used to travel in the coaches. They used to build a platform at The Wallows sheds specially for the Himley Fete trains. The line to the new shed, the asbestos one nearest the road, used to run between two walls, and they used to load the trains there.

After leaving the Navy I worked all around the country with heavy earth-moving equipment and that sort of thing. Then Round Oak advertised in the paper for a Diesel Engineer. I applied for the job, and got it. That was in 1955, and when I first started they hadn't got any diesel locomotives or cranes - the first machine to arrive was a Coles crane, followed by loco tests. They tried a Northern loco, a diesel hydraulic, and then the diesel electric. The engineer at the time, and myself, made a report on each of these locos after giving each of them a good trial. The engineer at the time was Mr.Whitfield and he asked me what I though would be best. I replied that the diesel electric loco would be best from a maintenance point of view - so we plumped for the diesel electric.

We had the loco on trial first of all, for a period of about six months, and then we bought it. Then the others followed on fairly quickly. However, when No.2 came it had a different engine in! No.s 2, 3 and 4 came together, then there was a gap after which the rest came at regular intervals. When No.5 came, we took No.1 aside and modified it to bring it up to the same standard as all the others. The second series had single traction motors, and were a source of a certain amount of trouble at first. The engine was too powerful and too heavy for its mountings - the mountings weren't resilient enough. We undertook our own modifications, putting shock absorbers on etc. The people from Paxmans came up to see how we had done it, as they had never tackled the problem themselves.

When I first arrived at Round Oak they still had about six steam locos working but gradually they withdrew them and scrapped them, apart from King George V which went off to Sheffield. The engine crews transferred to the diesels and I had to instruct them in their new task. When the shift came off they used to come into the shed and I would instruct them on diesel locomotive peculiarities, and simple things like checking the oil, and how to drive with the different controls, how to get the water out the air systems and all that sort of thing. They were conscientious men and were good drivers although some of them had worked with the steam engines for a long time. If you could tell them straight, in Black Country language, they could understand what was wanted of them.

All the diesels, apart from No.1, had heated cabs, so working on the diesels was a bit different to working on the steamers. The company had made the most out of its steamers. For example, when I first started work at Round Oak I noticed that when the steamers finished work and came on shed, they would drop their fires. They would drive over a pit and someone would rake out the fire. The company had a gleed wheeler - a man who used to collect the ashes and wash them in a big vat of water. Any ashes that floated were skimmed off and collected. They were taken over to the works and were burnt on the hearths where they were making chain. It shows you how frugal they were in those days.

Below: The Yorkshire Engine Co. diesel electric locomotives congregate at the Wallows on 27th May 1980 (Whit Monday). No.1., on the left, was the 1955 "precursor" of the fleet and had a slightly different cab to the rest of the locomotives Note the Hippodrome in the background, the running shed, and the wagon repair shed behind no.10. (Gordon Nutt)

An engine would be crewed by a driver and a shunter, and there were three shifts of drivers, and they all had to be trained bit by bit. They were quite impressed with the new diesels, especially when you consider the down time on the old steam engines - it could take six hours to fire them up from cold, and it was dirty work. You just had to go out to the diesel loco and press the button and it was ready for work, providing the maintenance was carried out. I had the engines inspected every day, on every shift more or less. They worked round the clock, and we used to swap them over one a week for a service.

From the start it was planned that we should have ten locos - one on stand by, one under repair, and eight at work. However it was a difficult scheme to maintain. Invariably, with breakdowns, we could usually keep seven locos at work: we could rarely manage a full complement of eight locos. The melting shops would take two or three locos, so there was easily enough work to keep the seven locos occupied. The melting shop locos would receive quite a hammering, particularly pulling the ingots out, and you could see their wheels slipping as they did so. When the steam locos used to fetch the ingots out of the casting bay into the soaking bay area, they used to attach two steamers. They could only employ the smaller steam locos on this work as there was such a sharp curve in the track. The new diesels had a short wheelbase, but only one was required to do the work of two steam locos.

The steam locomotives also had to work hard on the Barrow Hill Incline. They had to stand off at the bottom, perhaps about quarter of a mile back from the foot of the incline. They would race forward, propelling four to six wagons, dash up the incline, and the driver then had to shut off the regulator just as he hit the top of the incline. If he didn't, the water in the boiler would rush forward and drop the fusible plug in the firebox - and put the fire out.

When we went to Barrow Hill with the diesel for the first time, we were coming up the Incline and about half way up I told the driver to stop the loco. The driver went mad. "Bloody hell," he said, "you'll have it run away." However he stopped it, and then eased the regulator open a little. The wheels spun slightly so he put a little sand down, and then away she went - no trouble at all! You could also open the regulator, put the brakes on, let the engine build up power, and then ease the brake off. This was the sort of thing the blokes on the melting shop had to be taught - they would open the regulator, when putting the brake on would have stopped the wheel spin and provided a bit of traction.

The steam drivers had always dreadedrunning away on the Barrow Hill Incline because once or twice it had happened. There was a trap at the foot of the incline, running into the wood, and once or twice the steamers had ended up in the wood.

The diesels took over the shed that had been used by the steamers. It was as black as hell inside when we took over - you certainly couldn't see through any of the windows, but we had a crew of blokes to come in and clean it all down, and paint it. We installed a crane where they had once had a hydraulic crane, and we emptied the pit of copper pipes. As the tubes had been pulled out the boilers of the steam locos they had chucked them in the pit, and there were boxes and boilers everywhere - new ones - the place was cluttered right up. Trying to strip a diesel engine down in a place like that was hopeless, but it was fine once we had cleaned it all out. We bought lifts - sixty ton lifts to lift the bodies of the locos clear of the traction motors, to replace hydraulic jacks which had previously been used. It had been a really risky business - a jack at each corner, and timber used to pack up the body as we lifted it. We also had an new electric crane, and heaters.

We had offices at the back of the sheds, and I did all the ordering of spare parts. Normally at Round Oak everything had to bought by the Purchasing Department, but I could sidestep that, and I had authority to buy stuff as I saw fit, otherwise we could not have obtained spares quickly enough. The railway was in the hands of the Railway Engineer, but the running of the railway was in the hands of the Traffic Department.

The Traffic Department controlled all the drivers and shunters, and worked out the rosters for the locos, worked the shifts out etc., and that was done from a central point in the works. All the locos were fitted with intercom, and could be controlled from the Central Traffic Office. That was really the only way we could work the railway. Without the intercom it would have taken a lot of time to inform the blokes what they had to do. They just said, "Put 2 in No.6, Jack," and that was that. On the loco itself you had the driver, the shunter, and the shift traffic controller for that area of the works. The Traffic Department had a Transport Clerk, and he would have to control movement of wagons, and of road vehicles. The locos were fetching the coal from Baggeridge, servicing the steel plant, and fetching and returning wagons to and from the main line to keep the demurrage down, fetching work out of the bar finishing plant, and putting it in.

There was also the incline down to the rolling mills and stock yards at The Level. At one time this had been as steep as Barrow Hill, and locos were assisted with a steel rope, but the lower end of the incline was levelled out and modified, and the diesel locos could get up quite comfortably.

Our department had to maintain all sorts of equipment - fork lift trucks, cranes, dumper trucks and even concrete mixers, and we used to do the garage work as well, so we must have had at least twenty fitters and mates, and loco cleaners. They were mainly employees of longstanding, but we did start on our own apprentices and they were good. Some have gone on to do well since leaving Round Oak. One of the jobs we did was to rebuild a steam crane used at the coal wharf near The Wallows, and convert it to diesel, but unfortunately they did not use it for long after its conversion and it was scrapped. We also had to deal with engine "No.0". This was the company's first experiment with a diesel loco. They must have bought it in the days when nobody knew much about diesels. I was told that it had been built for work in a munitions factory.The company bought it to work in what was once the blast furnaces - it was down there when I found it! It was a diesel hydraulic, and it was a swine. It was a very small loco, and just wasn't up to the job at all. It couldn't tackle anything other than very light work. We had it in the sheds stripped down most of the time but we couldn't get it to work very well. It would stick in gear and almost rip its own gear box out. We did make it work for a while so they were going to take it into service, and they wondered what to call it. Some bright spark said, "Call it number nothing!" - so that's what happened, and "No.0" was painted on it. It was very aptly named. It went to the burners in the end. * (We also had a "No.11.", but that was simply painted onto the front of "No.1." after the engine was modified.)

"No.0" was the only diesel that we cut up for scrap, but the company did scrap all but one of the steam locomotives. We also cut up ex B.R. locomotives and tenders, and large numbers of wagons. Once we scrapped a loco brought in from a local gas works. A man came in who said he had spent his life driving that loco and he was sad to see it scrapped, so we gave him the nameplate. It is interesting to note that our diesels were sold to Round Oak Rail Ltd, and most of them survive - but I understand that they cannibalise some to keep others running.

Most people remember the bells fitted to our diesels, but they don't know the whole story. When new the locos had phosphor bronze bells which rang with a very melodious clang. Unfortunately these were stolen and we had to replace them with bells of aluminium brass - which rang with a distinctive "clonk".

("No.0" was a Robert Stephenson & Hawthorn 0-4-0, no.6979, built in 1940 for the Air Ministry's line at Quedgley. No.s 1 to 10 were Yorkshire Engine Co. 0-4-0 diesel electrics, with Paxman engines.)*

Right: Yorkshire Engine Co. diesel no.2 , featured again on the next page, is seen here on 21st September 1980, while still working for the steel works. The body has been lifted clear of the wheels and transmission by the powerful jacks, now "preserved" on the Severn Valley Railway. The "Hippodrome" seems to be a bright and modern workshop, but it dates back to 1938, and earned its nick name as it was built at the same time as the Dudley Hippodrome on Castle Hill. (Gordon Nutt)

Below: Another picture of work proceeding in the "Hippodrome" at the Wallows was taken on 9th July 1978 when no.10 and no.3 were receiving attention. (No.10 was Yorkshire Engine 2883 of 1962, and no.3 was 2662 of 1957.) The workshop had the services of an overhead crane as well as the jacks. On this occasion Bob Dignam and Pete Sant are seen at work. (Gordon Nutt)

Left: The nationalisation of the coal and steel industries, and the subsequent denationalisation of the latter, had some interesting effects on the Pensnett Railway. In 1952 the National Coal Board took over the running of the line from Askew Bridge and Baggeridge Junction to Baggeridge Colliery, and two new Hunslet 0-6-0STs were put into service. At Askew Bridge the coal wagons were handed over to the Round Oak Steel Works locomotives to continue their journey up the Barrow Incline and across to Round Oak. From 1962 onwards the new diesel locomotives made easy work of ascending the incline, but in 1966 the Steel Works decided that delivery of coal from Baggeridge by rail was no longer required. This picture was taken on 26th September 1966, at Askew Bridge, as NCB 0-6-0ST No. 9 (Hunslet 3777 of 1952) hands over to Round Oak Steel Works diesel no.10. for the last time, marking, in effect, the closure of the Pensnett Railway from Askew Bridge to the Wallows. (Collection of Viv Morgan)

Left: The survival of the Round Oak diesel locomotives is quite remarkable, now that all the other industrial locomotives of the Black Country have vanished from their work places - just as the work places themselves have disappeared. In this picture locomotive no.2 (Yorkshire Engine no.2614 of 1957) is propelling three Powell Duffryn covered cold-rolled steel wagons back into the new Round Oak Rail Terminal, on 20th August 1986, for the benefit of a video film unit. The terminal was officially opened on 3rd September 1986, and the diesels looked smart in their red and black stripes! Naturally there is not enough shunting to keep drivers fully employed on the footplate and the workforce at the terminal has to be "flexible" regarding their duties.

(Ned Williams)

Left: Seven years later we find that No.2 is still at work at Round Oak, but has turned round and gained the name "Excalibur"! Once again it is photographed propelling the Powell Duffryn wagons back into the terminal. On this occasion, the 15th March 1993, the wagons had been brought down to Round Oak from Bescot via Dudley - over the stretch of line that closed a few days later. On the left is Round Oak South signal box, which had officially closed in 1989, when its levers were brought under the control of the signalman at Kingswinford Junction. The use of the rail terminal involves bringing a shunter, or relief signalman, up from Kingswinford Junction to man the box while shunting and exchanging wagons with the Round Oak Rail Terminal engines. (Ned Williams)

Other Industrial Railways

Right: Gibbons (Dudley) Ltd. built a standard gauge railway in 1899 to run from their brickworks at Dibdale down to the Earl of Dudley's railway system near the foot of the Barrow Hill Incline. They purchased an Andrew Barclay 0-4-0ST (Works no. 847 of 1899) to run their railway, and in 1920 purchased a second Barclay 0-4-0ST (1653), which is illustrated here. The engines did not carry nameplates, but their names "Emily" and "Gibbons 1920" were painted on their side tanks. The line was abandoned in 1938, and sometime during the war both locomotives were sold to Cashmore's at Great Bridge.
(Collection of Viv Morgan)

Right: In 1913 the land and collieries once belonging to John Bradley, at Shut End, were purchased by Messrs H.S.Pitt & Co. Subsequently some of the pits were worked by Guy Pitt & Co., and "Peter" was purchased by that company in 1946, having previously worked at the Highley Mining Co.'s Kinlet Colliery. "Peter" was an 0-6-0ST built by Andrew Barclay (works no. 782 of 1896). It Salopian origins account for the fact that in 1969 it returned to Shropshire to become an exhibit in the Ironbridge Gorge Museum. In this 1960s view it is seen shunting the container wagons into the Pensnett trading Estate. "Peter" and "Winston Churchill" left their own tracks to venture over GWR metals through Pensnett Halt to gain access to Guy Pitt's colliery at Standhills, Kingswinford, from 1938 to 1947.
(Eric Rogers / Lawrence Brownhill)

Right: "Winston Churchill" (Manning Wardle 0-6-0ST 2025 of 1923) brings the container wagons into the Pensnett Trading Estate in 1961. Just as "Peter" returned to Shropshire, "Winston Churchill" was destined to retire to the Pensnett Trading Estate (see page 78).
(Viv Morgan)

Left: M & W Grazebrook Ltd built a standard gauge line in the 1870s running from the sidings on the GWR (ex OWWR) line at Blowers Green to the company's ironworks and pits. The company liked 0-4-0 STs built by Peckett of Bristol and "Grazebrook No.2" arrived new in 1938 (works no.1931), and worked on the line until its closure in 1962. "Grazebrook No.2" was then cut up on the site.
(Eric Rogers/Lawrence Brownhill)

Left: 0-4-0ST "Francis" (Peckett No. 1704 of 1927) was acquired new by M & W Grazebrook Ltd. and was used on the line at Blowers Green until being sold in 1961, a year before traffic ceased altogether. It is photographed here outside the engine shed, which could be seen easily from the point where the line crossed Cinder Bank on the level. The GWR "main line" is just behind the piles of timber seen in the distance to the left of the locomotive.
(Eric Rogers via Lawrence Brownhill)

Messrs Lunt Comley & Pitt opened their coal concentration depot at Pensnett on 1st May 1964, and in time this became the terminus, and reason for survival, of the line from Kingswinford Junction. In 1970 they purchased this 0-4-0 diesel electric locomotive from British Rail. (BR no. D2868). It was joined five years later by a sister (or "brother"?) engine, both products of the Yorkshire Engine Co. of 1960 vintage. "Sam" is seen here on 13th March 1986 in "retirement" and was apparently supplying spares to "Peter".
(Ned Williams)

The Railway at Dudley Zoo.

Dudley Zoo opened in 1937 and the Zoo management were looking for one or two attractions of a non-zoological nature to add to the zoo. At the time Trevor Guest, a director of the Stourbridge building contractors, A.H.Guest Ltd., had built a 10 1/4" gauge railway at the Crown Hotel at Wychbold, near Droitwich. The railway had two locomotives (both "Atlantics"), carriages and some track. A zoo director suggested that it be moved in its entirety to the zoo.

A syndicate was formed to run the railway in its new home in the zoo, and the principal shareholder in this syndicate was William Martin - a retired publican.(Other members of the syndicate were Trevor Guest and Captain Saunders.) Bill Martin took charge of the day to day running of the railway during its Easter to September running season. He even moved to a house in The Broadway to be nearer the zoo, but then moved to Cleobury Mortimer! His daughter Fay, who is still alive today, remembers that he travelled from there into Dudley each day to run the railway, often going via Stourbridge to pick up Joe Walkenden, a retired footplateman, who was one of the railway's drivers. (Joe Walkenden was a Londoner exiled to Stourbridge Shed, where he was a much respected railwayman. He retired at sixty and was glad of the opportunity to continue driving locomotives, and his example was followed by other drivers retiring from work at Stourbridge Shed, such as Frank Bellamy, and Harry Rampton.)

Trevor Guest would come along on Sunday afternoons in the early days of the railway's existence at the zoo, to drive the locomotive, but generally matters were left very much in the hands of Bill Martin, who sold the tickets, saw that passengers were properly seated in the train etc. During the school holidays Bill's son would help collect tickets, and another thing that the family remembers is the vast amount of cash brought home after a day's work during the Bank holiday weekends. The days were too hectic to find time to count the takings, let alone try and bank them! On such days huge queues built up of zoo-visitors anxious to take a ride on the little railway, and during the wartime summers it was busier than ever, as people were encouraged to take "holidays at home". For a time the two "atlantics" were supplemented by a 4-6-0 locomotive resembling a GWR "Saint".

It was difficult to maintain coal supplies to keep the line running during the war, so Trevor Guest built a railcar, powered by an old Singer petrol engine.

In 1946, as soon as the War was over, it was decided that the line could improve its capacity by being rebuilt from 10 1/4" gauge to 15" gauge. Trevor Guest set about building two large 4-6-0 locomotive to drawings produced by Ernest Twining, and with Goodhand boilers. As the first locomotive was completed it was realised that it might benefit from a larger firebox, so the second locomotive was modified in this way and was a 4-6-2. Both locomotives entered service at the zoo. The first was painted maroon, the second was painted in Caledonian blue.

Ernest Twining then produced drawings for a 2-4-2 locomotive, and this was also built and went into service at the zoo. It eventually received the name, "Katie", although planned as a "Sylvia", and later enjoyed fame on the Fairbourne Railway on the Welsh coast. The latter was owned by John Wilkins at the time, and he ordered a sister engine to "Katie" which was christened "Sian". While "Sian" was being built, the 4-6-0 from Dudley Zoo was loaned to the Fairbourne line where it was known as "Prince Charles". The 4-6-2 engine also left Dudley Zoo to go to Fairbourne when steam traction at the zoo was abandoned. John Wilkin's wish was that it should be named "Ernest Twining" after its designer.

Trevor Guest also built several petrol and diesel locomotives that found use on the Dudley Zoo railway. A "Bo-bo" locomotive, powered by a Daimler petrol engine was built in 1957, followed by a "Co-bo", powered by a Humber petrol engine in 1960. "Clara" was an 0-4-2T steam locomotive in outline, but was originally powered with a Petter diesel engine, later replaced with a Daimler petrol engine.

The railway had changed in its layout when re-gauged in 1946, and in its post-war period the trains ran into a single track station, with platforms on either side of the track. The locomotives did not run-round their train - the train was propelled on its outward journey, and pulled on the return journey. On the outward journey the driver had to stand on the footplate and peer over his train! Immediately on leaving the station the line passed through a tunnel, which doubled as a carriage shed, and then travelled along the eastern flank of Castle Hill for a few hundred yards, passing over a couple of bridges. There was no station or facilities at the outward end of the line.

At some stage the running of the railway passed to the Zoo's own control, and through-out the sixties it was operated with the petrol engine locomotives. It was operated under the Zoo's auspices for the last time in 1976.

In 1977 the line was operated by Messrs Wyatt & Tizard Ltd., who used a four - wheel petrol railcar. The new operator also demolished the sheds. The railway survived, in its new ownership, for four seasons, and when it was closed at the end of summer 1980, the track was lifted. Undaunted, some track was relaid in 1981 and Dudley Steam Railways took over. As the new operator's name implied, steam was about to return to the zoo's railway.A 4-4-2 locomotive built by Albert Barnes in 1925 (No. 105, "Michael") came to Dudley Zoo from Rhyl and propelled the train up and down a short length of track.

Even "Clara" reappeared on the system. By 1982 the track had been extended and the railway was almost its "old self" again. "Michael" was sent away for repairs and its place was taken by "Billie" - another Albert Barnes 4-4-2, No.104, this time from Margate. Unfortunately the steam revival only lasted until the end of the 1984 season. "Michael", "Billie" and "Clara" then went back to Rhyl.

The line's operation was then taken over by Rapido Rail Systems, who used a four wheel coach powered by a Lister diesel generator. This ran until the final closure of the line in September 1992. The Dudley Zoo Railway thus had quite a varied history and lasted for more than half a century.

Above: The miniature railway was featured in the zoo's publicity, and was given a "high profile" in the zoo in pre-war days. (On entering the zoo, visitors were confronted with a large notice board directing them to the railway!) In this posed photograph, the zoo's Indian elephant is brought along to admire one of the Trevor Guest 10 1/4" gauge 4-4-2s. Note that the platform arrangement is different to that seen in the picture at the top of the next page. (The elephant is believed to be "Maharanee" - sold to Robert Brothers Circus in 1946.) (Collection of Fay Davis)

Top left: Schoolboys line the station fence to admire the "Saint" class locomotive on Dudley Zoo's railway in 1939. Twining's 4-6-0 based on the outlines of the GWR locomotives of the Saint class carries the number "3" and was supplied to assist the two 4-4-2 locomotives built by Trevor Guest for the 10 1/4" gauge line. Note the track layout seems to have gone through some modification since the "elephant" photograph, and an island platform seems to occupy the site of the original loop.
(Collection of Hugh Sykes)

Middle left: At the other end of the railway's life, the 15" gauge 4-4-2 built by Barnes, No.104 of 1928, waits to leave the carriage shed on 12th June 1983.
(John Williams)

Bottom left: The Bo-Bo locomotive, built in 1957 by Trevor Guest, and powered by a Daimler petrol engine, looks very smart as it stands on its train by the "new" carriage shed, built over the running lines.
(Hugh Sykes)

Above right: Driver Bill O'Rourke inspects No.104, the Barnes 4-4-2 of 1928 vintage, while waiting to depart by propelling his train out of the two-platformed station on 12th June 1983 - during the 1980's steam revival on the line. It is tempting to assume the words "Zoo Railway" on the signal gantry were transferred from the side of the engine shed, as seen in the earlier photos. The left hand platform was used for unloading, the right hand for loading.
(John Williams)

Above and midddle right: Three pictures of post-war motive power on the Zoo Railway. A Guest 4-6-0 and "Katie" are both photographed by the water tank, but the GWR style railcar is only glimpsed in the shed. Note changes to the track layout and the re-positioning of the "Zoo Railway" lettering from the gantry to the side of the shed. In the picture of "Katie" two wooden "girders" from one of the bridges at the far end of the line are "resting" by the new pointwork.
(Eric Rogers / Lawrence Brownhill)

Bottom right: Many people's memories of the Zoo Railway feature "Clara", the 0-4-2T internal combustion engine powered locomotive built by Trevor Guest to remotely resemble the popular GWR 14XX steam locomotives of the same wheel arrangement. (Collection of Hugh Sykes)

Left: A bright new future for the Black Country? The monorail at the Merry Hill Centre links the centre of the shopping complex with the offices built on "The Waterfront" site. The Swiss-built £21m system took three years to construct and opened in June 1991 after satisfying stringent tests and requirements of the Railway Inspectorate. You might not feel it is a "railway", but it is "public transport" and visitors to the Black Country who arrive at Merry Hill via the upper road from Round Oak are often very impressed with the sight of the monorail's sleek trains gliding over the gentle switchback down into the shopping centre. There is little in the landscape to remind visitors that this new development has been built in an area that was once the back of Round Oak Steel Works, served by the Earl of Dudley's railway system, but if you travel to the Waterfront by monorail, leave the station, cross the road and scale the new embankment you can look into the backyard of the Round Oak Steel Terminal, and catch a glimpse of the surviving Round Oak diesel locomotives still at work!

(Ned Williams)

Left: One of the Black Country's most short-lived railways was a short stretch of line installed at the Black Country Museum in 1991 as part of a "steam" event. Ex B.R. (N.E. Region) J72 0-6-0T 69023 "Joem" ran, without any "train" or passenger carrying facilities, up and down this length of track for a few weeks. School parties visiting the Museum at the time were offered footplate visits, but no photographic opportunities were exploited, and it did not represent any move by the Museum towards preserving railway artefacts as part of their picture of the Black Country's past. (Ned Williams)

Left: 0-6-0ST "Winston Churchill" stands on a short length of track in the Pensnett Trading Estate, photographed here on 13 March 1986. The locomotive, built by Manning Wardle in 1923 (works no. 2025), was acquired by Guy Pitt & Co. for work at Shut End in 1946, when it was given its name. It survived to work the traffic on the Pensnett Trading Estate's railway, and was last steamed in 1968. In 1970 it was taken to the site of the Black Country Museum where it stood at the Tipton Road/New Road cross roads for several years before returning to Pensnett.

(Ned Williams)

Above: Class 47 locomotive, 47 238, passes Wednesbury signal box at Potters Lane on 19 March 1993 with the last Bescot - Brierley Hill (Moor Lane) Steel Terminal "trip" working to travel via Dudley. On this day the railway from Bescot to Round Oak, via Wednesbury, Great Bridge, and Dudley, effectively closed. To mark the occasion the locomotive, named "Bescot Yard", is carrying two head boards: "The Pensnett Knocker" and "The Dudley Dasher Memorial Special". The photograph is taken from the abutment of the overbridge carrying the former GWR Birmingham - Wolverhampton main line. As well as Wednesbury Town station disappearing from this view (once on the far side of Potters Lane), other local landmarks such as St.John's Church have also vanished! (Ned Williams)

Below: Towards the end of the afternoon on 19 March 1993, 47 238, "Bescot Yard" returns with the trip working from Brierley Hill to Bescot via Dudley. Still carrying the headboard, "The Dudley Dasher Memorial Special", the locomotive waits at the signal guarding the approach to Eagle Crossing, Great Bridge. On the left are the empty sidings of Great Bridge Yard, which once enjoyed canal interchange facilities, and had recently enjoyed some use as a depot for Mercury telecommunications work. Although anxious to be the "last train" over the line, this train was followed by a further light engine movement! Although recovery of the track was one of the reasons given for closing the line, the track has remained in place until now (the summer of 94). Traffic to Brierley Hill, Pensnett, and Round Oak now travels via Stourbridge Junctio n. (Ned Williams)

Other books available from Uralia Press

Pat Collins - King of Showmen

Freda Allen & Ned Williams

A biography of the Black Country's famous showman. This book not only tells the amazing story of Pat's life, from the fairground to the House of Commons, but also describes his fairground equipment, the shows, the amusement parks, his organs, engines, the people he worked with, and the fairs he presented. Profusely illustrated.

264 pp. A4 hardback. £15.

Fairs and Circuses in the Black Country

Ned Williams

The story of travelling entertainment; fairs, circuses, and shows, making their way through the Black Country. Meet Wolverhampton's great circus proprietor, ponder the words of the World's Fair's very own Black Country correspondent, and marvel at the vitality and variety of showland past and present. Many illustrations including over a dozen in colour.

96pp. A4 paperback £9.99.

The Co-op in Birmingham & the Black Country

Ned Williams

The Co-op is celebrating its 150th birthday in 1994, and this book marks the occasion by telling the story of six major local Co-operative societies, plus other smaller societies and productive organisations. Read about the shops, the transport, the struggles and successes of the people who worked together as members, staff, and customers - plus all the social activities pursued in the name of Co-operation. Over 200 illustrations, including some in colour.

200 pp. A4. hardback £15, paperback £9.99.

Plus limited supplies of our older publications:

Shop in the Black Country

Ned Williams

Over 200 pictures, plus 25 in colour, of local shops, portraying their design, their history, and the style in which they have traded, from the 1880s to the 1980s, from corner shops to mighty multiples.

72 pp. A4. paperback £4.95.

The Railway to Wombourn

Ned Williams

A well illustrated account of the GWR branch line that ran from Oxley Junction, outside Wolverhampton, to Kingswinford Junction, via Wombourn. Part of the line served pits, brickworks etc in fine Black Country style, while the other half served rural south Staffordshire.

64 pp. A4. paperback £4.95.

Wolverhampton on Wheels

Ned Williams and Simon Dewey

Nearly 100 photographs, and a full colour cover, bring you the excitement and variety of Wolverhampton's road and rail history - from horse drawn Co-op bakery vans to mighty steam locomotives - Wolverhampton built such things. Includes buses, trams, trolleys, bikes, motorcycles, commercial vehicles and trains.

96pp. 2/3 A4 paperback. £4.50

Black Country Folk at Werk and More Black Country Folk at Werk

Ned Williams

Local people recall their working lives, and the whole world of "werk" comes to life in their own words - covering a great variety of "werk" experience, both in trades traditionally associated with the Black Country, and in some more unusual ways of earning a living.

Each book is a 96 pp A4 paperback.

Originally £5.95. each - now available direct from Uralia Press only at a special offer price of £6 the pair.

All books can be supplied by post, but please add 10% towards the cost of postage. (Orders over £30 in value sent post free.) Cheques payable to Uralia Press.

Uralia Press
23 Westland Road
Wolverhampton WV3 9NZ

Work in progress - future plans:
All information, help, photographs etc... gratefully received concerning Black Country transport, shops, theatres, cinemas, trade union banners and Co-op history. Further information always sought about local fairs, and showland families, circuses etc.

The Black Country Society

The society brings together people from all walks of life who share an interest in the past, present and future of the Black Country. Regular meetings are held at four separate centres, a high quality quarterly magazine is sent to all members, and the society organises a programme of weekly walks each summer exploring the region. There are also special events ranging from festivals at the Black Country Museum to Christmas Carol Concerts presented in a unique Black Country style. Members can purchase certain books on local matters at discount prices, and have the chance to join fellow enthusiasts working on industrial archeology, book publishing, and photography. Enquiries should be addressed to the membership secretary - Ron Julian, 97 Stream Road, Kingswinford, DY6 0HR.